SAVING THE
CUMBRES & TOLTEC
~SCENIC~
RAILROAD

For Debbie and Bob
with best wishes!

Spencer Wilson

SPENCER WILSON
WES PFARNER, PHOTO ARCHIVIST

Wes Pfarner

Charleston ‖‖ London

THE
History
PRESS

Published by The History Press
Charleston, SC 29403
www.historypress.net

Cover image by Tom Barrows.

All images are from the Richard L. Dorman Collection unless otherwise noted.

First published 2012

Manufactured in the United States

ISBN 978.1.60949.547.3

Library of Congress CIP data applied for.

CONTENTS

PREFACE

The Cumbres & Toltec Scenic Railroad (C&TS) has been a tourist operation for more than thirty-five years. The sixty-four miles of the former San Juan Extension of the Denver & Rio Grande Western (D&RGW) Railway was saved three times by volunteers and remain vital and powerful reminders of New Mexico's and Colorado's great railroading past. The railroad is also a testimony to the two groups of volunteers that worked tirelessly to preserve it for succeeding generations. The purpose of this book is to tell the story of the volunteers, the history of the C&TSRR and the personal involvement of the author, beginning in 1974.

The states of Colorado and New Mexico bought the sixty-four miles of narrow-gauge railroad between Chama, New Mexico, and Antonito, Colorado, in 1970. This was a complicated effort, starting with volunteers and far-seeing politicians in both states, and culminated in a joint agreement to purchase the railroad's right-of-way, rails, buildings and rail cars, also known as rolling stock. Early volunteers were also part of a continuing effort to preserve and repair the historic structures and the rolling stock. The first volunteer effort ultimately failed and, in time, was replaced by a far more successful organization.

The two state legislatures were influenced to appropriate the funds for the railroad's purchase for two essential reasons. One was to stimulate the tourism industries in two of the poorer counties in each state. Rio Arriba County in northern New Mexico and Conejos County in southern

Colorado ranked close to the bottom of the economic scale. A second and perhaps more idealistic reason was to preserve a vanishing form of the once vital railroad industry—especially the coal-fired, steam-powered locomotives, which by then were long gone from mainline railroads throughout the United States and most other parts of the world. The hope was that the operation of a historic railroad would be a great tourist attraction. The hope was not in vain, as it turned out, and a measure of tourism prosperity was brought to these more remote mountain areas. Thus was born the Cumbres & Toltec Scenic Railroad.

Volunteers saved the railroad, operated a few of the early excursions and continued to play secondary roles after a regular operator was chosen. Then the group fell on hard times and ultimately ceased to exist. A new and far more successful volunteer group appeared by the early 1980s, providing manpower, money and materials to preserve the rolling stock and structures that had not been used by the first post-1970 operator.

That latter volunteer group matured as the historic preservation arm of the C&TS, emerging in 1988 as the Friends of the C&TSRR Inc. In the last year of the old century, developments on the railroad again threatened the very existence of the line with abandonment. The Friends, as volunteers, once again stepped in with manpower, money and materials to ensure the continuous operation of this historic railroad. On April 1, 2000, the Friends entered into a five-year contract to operate the trains. For the third time in three decades, volunteers again saved this icon of western heritage.

It is also hoped that this book will serve as a guide to other volunteer groups to avoid the pitfalls and failures that can plague such volunteer efforts so that the success of hard work, dedicated charity and dynamic volunteerism can be measured time and again.

This book is dedicated to the past, present and future members of the Friends of the Cumbres & Toltec Scenic Railroad and to those others who helped make this treasure of transportation both a tourism reality and an enduring and fully operational relic of New Mexico's and Colorado's historic pasts. The exploits of many of these preservationists are described on the following pages. My thanks to those who read the manuscript: Vernon Glover, Wes Pfarner, Tim Tennant, Howard Bunte and William J. Lock.

Author's note: Asterisks present in chapters indicate a note of explanation to be featured later in the "Notes" chapter at the end of this book.

CHAPTER 1

BACKGROUND

The Cumbres & Toltec Scenic Railroad is the direct descendant of the Denver & Rio Grande (D&RG), a railroad company chartered in Denver in 1870 with the ambition of building a line from Denver to Mexico City, with a branch line to the Pacific coast of Mexico. A Civil War veteran, General William Jackson Palmer, organized that project. General Palmer had risen to the command of the 15th Pennsylvania Volunteer Cavalry Regiment during the Civil War and, like so many veterans of both the North and South, migrated west after the war to Denver.

Located at the base of the Rocky Mountains, Denver was already a center of activity for the gold mines opening up farther into the mountains. However, the only means of transporting people, building materials, food and other supplies were stagecoaches and wagons. They were not only slow and very uncomfortable in mountain terrain—passengers often became "seasick" riding in the coaches—but they were also very expensive for shipping freight. Denver lacked a railroad to ship gold ore out and bring in the needed supplies.

By 1870, Denver did have a railroad connection to the Union Pacific at Cheyenne, Wyoming, and a second road, the Kansas Pacific, had been built across the prairie to Denver from Kansas. But these were not enough to satisfy the ambitions of a town growing with the lure of all of the mines to the west. Denver needed railroads reaching in every direction. One such direction was to the south, from Denver to Santa Fe in the

New Mexico Territory and then, perhaps, on to Mexico City. In October 1870, the Denver & Rio Grande Railway was born.

General Palmer was a railroader by training. Early in life, he worked for eastern railroads, studied railways and mining in England and prepared for a career in railroads. During the Civil War, Palmer served with distinction, rising from captain to general and winning the Medal of Honor. After the war, he went west to survey railroad routes to the Pacific Ocean and supervised the building of the Kansas Pacific Railroad into Denver. Palmer was both builder and promoter. The ability to attract capital from eastern and European sources was vitally important to any railroad project, and Palmer was as adept at fundraising as at railroad building.

Palmer dreamed of a railroad going south from Denver along the eastern side of the Rocky Mountains, up over Raton Pass and into New Mexico. He envisioned that it would extend farther south to Santa Fe, follow the Rio Grande into Mexico and then go to Mexico City, with an extension to the Pacific on the Gulf of California. Almost all projected railroads of that day dreamed of reaching the Pacific coast, hoping to tap into the lucrative China trade. Most never got there. Palmer's dream also succumbed to changing circumstances.

During his studies and travels, Palmer was influenced by technical developments affecting railroads that he observed in England, where modern railroading had begun during the early nineteenth century. A major issue was the establishment of gauges, or the width between tracks, as practiced by the English. Many later American railroads had adopted the British gauge of four feet and eight and a half inches. Both English and American railroads experimented with different gauges. The English were concerned about building railroads in the far reaches of their empire—and building them faster and cheaper. As a result of studies and experience, the English built many railroads with a three-foot distance between rails. There were many other widths in use at one time, but the three-foot gauge became a "standard" for narrow-gauge roads, just as four feet and eight and a half inches became "standard" gauge for most modern systems. Palmer also opted for the three-foot gauge, believing that, in mountains, construction would be cheaper due to narrower roadbeds, sharper curves and steeper grades. Indeed, railroad engineers argued the merits of narrow versus the wider gauges with charts and graphs. Within a few years, the advantages of the wider gauge were evident. Palmer, however, built his road to narrow-gauge parameters.

At the time, the industry at large had not anticipated the increased sizes of standard-gauge rolling stock and much more powerful locomotives. The railroad companies also had not anticipated the economic advantage of allowing the use of other companies' rolling stock on their own rails. This development was called "interchanging" and is practiced down to the present moment as rolling stock is consigned to other rail outfits and varying company logos can be seen on a single train. During the first part of the 1890s, the D&RG company began to widen its mainlines to the standard of four feet and eight and a half inches. Many of the narrow-gauge lines, such as the present C&TS Railroad, were never widened, since the cost of such reconstruction in rugged mountains with declining freight traffic outweighed the advantages. The outmoding of the narrow gauge was in the not-so-distant future, even as the "Baby Road," as the southern extension was called, was under construction south from Denver.

The railroads made a profit from hauling goods and people and, in many instances, from a contract with the U.S. Post Office to carry the mail. Every mile of rail cost money, which had to be raised through various means, including selling stock and borrowing money to finance construction. The companies also profited by becoming the nineteenth-century equivalents of modern land developers. The railroad acquired land titles in advance of construction, by purchase, government grants or by more devious means. Then the company laid out, or "platted," a town-site, laid the rails to and through the site and sold town lots.

The administrations of existing towns were often asked for cash or land as enticements for the railroad to locate through those areas. If towns did not offer such inducements, they faced a dim future, for being served by the railroad often meant life or death for a town. For instance, in building south from Denver, the D&RG laid out a new town called Colorado Springs, and within a short period, 2,500 people lived there. A collection of Ute Indians and eastern squatters at Colorado City was bypassed, and that town soon died. Service to the new town from Denver began on January 1, 1872, with the locomotive Montezuma pulling the diminutive thirty-five-foot cars of two compartments, each with two seats on one side and one seat on the other, with alternate arrangements in the second compartment—all to balance the weight of riders evenly. The D&RG was in business.

General Palmer's ambitions of building south into New Mexico Territory soon ran afoul of another equally ambitious railroad. The Atchison, Topeka and Santa Fe Railroad laid track west from Kansas through southern Colorado with the aim of traversing New Mexico to the Pacific coast. Both companies coveted the route through New Mexico down the Rio Grande. Both companies also wanted the best-known and most feasible route over the mountains separating Colorado and New Mexico, which was Raton Pass. The wagon road over Raton Pass was already well known as the route of the Santa Fe Trail, which had been in use since 1821. Now both railroads went after it. The Santa Fe won by being the first to start construction. This action cut General Palmer's "Baby Road" off from the easiest route into and through New Mexico. The general was not yet beaten, however.

Palmer turned his line west from Pueblo, Colorado, building through the Front Range of the Rocky Mountain chain in order to arrive at the booming mining area of Leadville, Colorado. Here the Atchison line again contested the most feasible route, which was through the canyon of the Arkansas River now called the Royal Gorge. A legal battle, and some violence, left the issue in doubt—with the Atchison again seemingly the winner. A series of lawsuits, court decisions and finally an agreement, the so-called Treaty of Boston, left Palmer in control of that vital passage. His road was built into the rich mining area. The Boston agreement also divided the territories between the two roads, which had the effect of prohibiting the D&RG from building into Santa Fe, New Mexico. Palmer had to look elsewhere for potential markets for his road.

Some of those potential markets turned out to be the San Juan Mountains of southwestern Colorado around the present cities of Durango and Silverton. This meant the construction of the present railroad from Antonito, Colorado, to Chama, New Mexico, and on to the west and back into Colorado. When construction began in 1880, the company's official name for the Antonito–Durango line was the San Juan Extension. The line was built as a narrow-gauge railroad.

The coming of the D&RG meant that boom times had arrived in southern Colorado and northern New Mexico. Miners, merchants, lumberjacks, cattle and sheep men, as well as all the hangers-on typical of boomtowns, flocked to the area. Antonito, Colorado, replaced the earlier town of Conejos and went on to become an important junction after the new town was built. At Antonito, the line split, with the San Juan Extension heading west and a branch line extending southward into New Mexico. This branch did not go more than seventy-five miles south of Antonito because of the Treaty of Boston. In later years, the D&RG did finally reach Santa Fe.

Chama became a rail center with extensive facilities to service the locomotives needed for the hard pull eastward up to Cumbres Pass. Chama grew from a small village to a good-sized town, with hotels, restaurants and homes for the railroad workers, and it became a mercantile center for the surrounding area. Boom times had arrived.

The San Juan Extension was built through the rugged southern Rocky Mountains, utilizing tunnels and bridges, including the highest bridge on the line, and much gradual gradation around the mesas and mountains to gain the height of Cumbres Pass at 10,015 feet above sea level. Railroads, then and now, must not attempt too steep a climb. Metal wheels on metal rails do not have the gripping ability of rubber tires on asphalt pavement. A grade that is too steep will cause slipping or reduce the numbers of cars being hauled by the locomotive to the point that the trains are so short that they are uneconomical. Even using two or three locomotives did not double the size of the train on such steep grades. The grade from Chama eastward to Cumbres Pass is rated at 4 percent for most of the fourteen miles. A 4 percent grade means that four feet of elevation is gained for every one hundred feet of travel. So when there was enough room, the builders utilized long loops to reduce the grade as much as possible, as in the route from Antonito to Cumbres Pass.

The San Juan Extension was in business in early 1881, and the line was busy. As soon as Durango and Silverton were reached, the trains carried a variety of freight and passengers into the area and the rich silver ores out. At one point during the boom years, management even contemplated widening the line over Cumbres Pass to a standard gauge, but that was never done. The silver boom in the American West did not last. In the 1880s and into the early 1890s, the U.S. Treasury bought silver for coinage. At the time, the United States was using both gold and silver as currency, but it became a hot political issue. By 1893, the "gold bugs" (proponents of using only gold for currency) had finally won. Congress stopped buying silver, the price collapsed and mining the metal came to a virtual halt. With the silver business ended, the railroad declined drastically. There was still enough freight, cattle, sheep, timber and passengers—along with the mail contract—to run daily trains. But the boom was over.

The railroad over Cumbres continued to be active on into the twentieth century. The company even modernized some rolling stock. New, larger and more powerful locomotives, such as the #463, were purchased as the older and smaller units were retired and scrapped. In the 1920s, even larger locomotives were added, represented by the #480s and #490s that power most of the trains today. In 1923, a larger, steam-powered rotary snowplow was bought to help keep the line open during the severe winters on Cumbres Pass. At various times, heavier steel rails were laid, but money was never available to do the expensive overhaul of widening the rails to standard gauge. So the trains and crews worked on, albeit with diminishing passenger traffic though supported by steady amounts of freight, lumber, cattle, sheep and, in the 1930s, important oil

The Chama oil dock is depicted with more than a dozen tank cars in sight. John Barriger took this photograph in 1938, looking west, showing close-up detail of the oil dock. Oil was piped to this location from Chromo in Archuleta County, Colorado, and then loaded at Chama in New Mexico and shipped back into Colorado, to Alamosa.

shipments from the Gramps oil field near Chama to a refinery in Alamosa, Colorado. For many years, the D&RG also ran a luxury passenger train, known as the San Juan Express, with a sleeper and parlor-restaurant car, but this was discontinued in 1951.

The end was in sight after World War II. Passengers left the trains for their automobiles, freight went to trucks and even the mail contract was hardly enough to justify running the trains. In 1951, the U.S. mail contract was dropped. The Interstate Commerce Commission (ICC) allowed the company to discontinue the San Juan Express, and no more passengers rode the "Baby Road" across Cumbres Pass. Freight shipments to the oil and gas fields of northwest New Mexico continued, along with lumber, crude oil and livestock. This business provided enough revenue for the line to continue operations.

By 1967, however, even this business declined to the point that only few trains ran. That decline resulted in the line—then known as the Denver & Rio Grande Western—applying to the ICC to abandon all service. The application was granted in 1968. It appeared to be the end. Abandonment meant that the rails would be taken up and turned into scrap steel, the rolling stock sold or scrapped and the line completely abandoned. Generally, when the rails were "lifted," the land in the old right-of-way reverted to public or private ownership. Almost all of the other narrow-gauge lines had already succumbed to the scrappers, with only the Alamosa–Silverton line remaining. A once vital and extensive railroad seemed dead.

In 1968, the railroad from Alamosa to Silverton was the last remnant of more than five hundred miles of narrow-gauge railroads in Colorado and New Mexico. It had remained narrow gauge even after the mainlines and some shorter lines were converted to standard gauge. As late as the 1940s, the traveler could ride the narrow-gauge "circle." By utilizing the Rio Grande Southern, an independent line that for years was owned by the D&RGW and ran from Durango to Ridgway, Colorado, a person could travel from Salida through Alamosa down to Chama and over to Durango. Then the traveler rode the Rio Grande Southern from Durango to Dolores and Telluride and on to Ridgway. From there, he or she could proceed by narrow-gauge passenger train through the Black Canyon of the Gunnison River and to the town of Gunnison and over Monarch Pass, completing the "circle" to the starting point at Salida.

These miles of narrow-gauge mainlines did not take into account the many miles of branch lines that ran into the mountains and valleys of the two states. These branch lines made possible the exploitation of raw materials, such as lumber and ores, as well as cattle and sheep shipments sent to markets elsewhere. Daily trains, both local and mainline, brought passengers, the mail and industrial goods from the east into the same remote towns, mining and lumber camps and ranching operations. There were even circus trains that visited the isolated communities. The railroads built telegraph lines for their own operational use and allowed local newspapers to connect to them—often via a wire from the depot to the newspaper office. The rails and the wires provided a window to the rest of the world. Isolation was a fact of mountain life until the coming of the rails.

After World War II, however, the narrow-gauge railroads began to decline. The world of the railroad industry was changing throughout the

A special double-headed passenger train, meaning one with two engines, is pulled by a T-12-class helper engine and a K-27-class road engine by the Chama depot. A large crowd of people gathered. This Kelly Collection photograph is estimated to have been taken in 1910.

nation, and not for the better. For one thing, the mines and timber sources were worked out, shipments by rail were shifting to trucks and passengers were leaving for automobiles and airplanes. Much of this exodus can be attributed to heavy-handed federal regulation, which dated from the creation of the ICC in the 1880s and even greater regulation during and after World War I.

When the United States entered that war, the railroads were overwhelmed. Wartime shipments were simply not getting through to the East Coast for transshipment to Europe. Some materials were even sent by truck on primitive roads of the day. As a result of this bottleneck, the federal government took over control of the railroads and never really let go until decades later. Thus, using the ICC, federal control hampered the rail industry, which was increasingly faced with truck and highway competition in the 1920s and 1930s. Railroads were forced to continue unprofitable trains and routes without being allowed to make rate changes or drop those unprofitable lines. The ICC set rates, making it impossible to compete, forcing the railroads to bear the expense of running unprofitable trains.

Furthermore, new technology in locomotives appeared to dim the future of steam power on narrow-gauge routes. By the 1930s, diesel engines had begun replacing steam on American railroads. Although steam continued into the 1950s, the advent of diesel-electric locomotives spelled doom for an older technology. At one point, the D&RGW experimented with small diesel locomotives for the narrow gauge, but they proved too small.

In those same decades, both the state and federal governments began the "farm to market" road building, which evolved into highway systems, subsidized by public money and free to the traveler and to commerce. Trucks were unregulated, and independent truckers began to make serious dents in the railroad business. Furthermore, the railroads were not allowed to diversify their business. After World War II, one railroad operated an airline, but the ICC soon forced it to abandon the flight business. Of course, during World War II, the railroads did a booming business, but that changed after the conflict. Unregulated competition of road and air began to cut into rail profits. In the 1950s, the Eisenhower administration even took the transport of U.S. mail off the rails in favor of trucks on the newly constructed and expanding interstate system.

A northbound freight train en route from Santa Fe on the "Chili Line" stops at Antonito, Colorado. This undated photo was taken by Otto C. Perry.

Rails were out, and cars, trucks and airplanes were in. Rail companies did apply to abandon unprofitable lines and were occasionally given permission to do so. In Colorado and New Mexico, especially with the narrow gauge, lines were closed and the rails taken up. As early as 1941, the "Chili Line" from Antonito, Colorado, to Santa Fe, New Mexico, was abandoned. It was a harbinger of the future.

In the 1980s, Congress finally deregulated the railroads. This action opened new markets to rail and made competition with trucks possible and profitable. It was, however, too late for the narrow-gauge roads of northern New Mexico and southern Colorado. When in 1968, the D&RGW petitioned the ICC to abandon the last remaining narrow-gauge route (save for the Durango–Silverton portion), the time was ripe for voices to be raised to "preserve the narrow gauge!"

The narrow gauge at stake, of course, represented the last remaining miles of the once extensive railroad network in Colorado and New Mexico. This last operation ran from Alamosa, Colorado, in the San Luis Valley, crossing the state border some eleven times, into Chama, New Mexico. From that point, the rails ran farther west to Durango and then split, one line north to Silverton and the other south to Farmington, New Mexico. This was still an active rail line, with trains traversing the line two or three times per week. ICC rules held that this service must continue. That rule meant a relocation project, with fateful results for the Chama–Antonito segment of the D&RGW.

This part of the story begins with a news item. On October 27, 1960, a news release buried inside the pages of the *Albuquerque Journal* caught the eye of Carl Turner, then executive director of the New Mexico Rural Electric Cooperative Association and, much later, twice member of the C&TSRR Commission. Turner was not a rail fan, railroad historian or model railroad builder. The item interested him because of any possible impact the matter might have on business for the local electric cooperative. Little could Turner—or anyone else, for that matter—predict the eventual results of that article in the newspaper.

The *Journal* reported that the U.S. Department of the Interior had just signed a contract with the Denver & Rio Grande Western Railroad. This contract provided for the relocation of about twelve miles of the line, nearly eight miles of country roads and the Western Union Telegraph Company's line in Archuleta County, Colorado. All were located within the area to be flooded by the Navajo Dam and Reservoir.

The Denver & Rio Grande Western engines #496 and #495 haul freight toward Cumbres Pass in the 1960s.

The Navajo Reservoir was a part of the much larger Colorado River Storage Project, scheduled for completion in 1963. The Navajo Dam was located on the San Juan River in San Juan and Rio Arriba Counties in northwest New Mexico. The lake formed by the dam would, when filled, extend back up the San Juan River into southwestern Colorado and inundate the roadbed of the narrow-gauge Denver & Rio Grande Western Railroad. Hence, there was a need to relocate that still active portion of the San Juan Extension of the parent railroad company. The filling of the reservoir also forced the relocation of a portion of the town of Arboles, Colorado. This relocation was not included in the contract between the federal agency and the railroad company.

According to the article, and a copy of the contract, the relocation would include a new roadbed, bridges and track for 12.2 miles of narrow-gauge, single-track railroad and about seven miles of county roads and structures. The work required "two steel-girder railroad bridges and one steel-girder, wood-deck Road Bridge." The low bidder was H.E. Lowdermilk Company of Englewood, Colorado, at $916,790. This was cheaper than any of the other nine bids received. A second contract was signed on February 27, 1962, providing for the D&RGW to supply the materials necessary to complete the project, including ties, spikes, bolts, switches and rails. The 1962 price of standard gauge ties was $3.50 apiece (as opposed to the 1995 price of about $18 per tie). The department promised to reimburse the D&RGW for the costs of rails, joints, switches and so forth over a five-year period, with payments to be made yearly starting with the date the new line was put into operation.

The second contract also specified that the Department of the Interior would assume all "deferred construction" over the new line. The department was aware that the new line would not be as stable as the former line and acknowledged that "the railroad operation over the relocated line during the seasoning period, especially new embankments, through raw cuts, and over new roadbed imposes extraordinary maintenance condition until the seasoning period is completed." Therefore, the government was also obligated for a period of five years to make annual payments to the railroad for "all that part of the cost and expense of extraordinary maintenance of the segments of the relocated line which can be attributed to lack of seasoning." These agreements had the effect of ensuring continued operation of the railroad for the agreed five years.

Background

The new line was officially put in operation at 8:00 a.m. on August 27, 1962, and continued to operate for those five years. On September 18, 1967, however, less than a month after the final federal payment, the D&RGW petitioned the ICC to abandon the entire narrow-gauge line, with the exception of the prosperous Durango–Silverton portion. That section was, by then, a moneymaking tourist operation, and the ICC refused the company's request to abandon it. The remaining narrow gauge from Farmington and Durango through Chama to Alamosa appeared doomed.

The stage was set for Carl Turner to remember the 1960 article, to wonder and then to act. He and like-minded businessmen in Chama, such as Joe and Eddie Vigil, began talking about saving the narrow gauge. They and others called for a meeting in Farmington, New Mexico, of the Four Corners Commission, with Turner presiding. This meeting included the San Juan County Commission and Clarence Quinlan, a like-minded member of the Colorado legislature from Antonito, Colorado. The Farmington meeting resulted in, among other things, the printing of bumper stickers that read, "Save the Narrow Gauge." The members also formed the committee to "Save the Narrow Gauge." A representative of the D&RGW was also in attendance and answered a question about the purchase price by saying, "You can buy the railroad for the change in my pocket." He rattled what coins were in his pocket. Subsequently, Governor Jack Campbell of New Mexico, Turner and "Duke" Mayshank, the governor's administrative assistant, traveled to Denver to meet with their equivalents there. The upshot of that meeting was the agreement to not oppose abandonment if the D&RGW would agree to sell.

A key figure in the New Mexico legislature at the time was John Mershon, chairman of the House Appropriations Committee. At a meeting in La Fonda Hotel in Santa Fe, this informal group decided to ask for $1,000 from the legislature. It was granted $100. This was a rather inauspicious beginning. It was going to take a lot more than one meeting of a few interested folks and a few coins to preserve this unique example of our patrimony. Carl Turner went on to other matters pertaining to the rural electric cooperatives. He did, however, retain an active interest in preserving the narrow gauge. Clarence Quinlan returned to Antonito to begin rallying support in Colorado. New Mexicans started organizing.

The San Juan Express passenger train, headed eastbound in 1938, crosses the Lobato Trestle. Lobato, located five miles north of Chama, near the Colorado line, is the site of 1,160 feet of siding, stock pens and the steel Lobato Trestle on the San Juan extension. The siding site is occasionally called "Weed City," referring to the fictional town name on a fake depot and water tank set up for the Gregory Peck western *Shoot Out* (1971). The stock pens are authentic structures from the Rio Grande era.

The official request by the D&RGW to abandon the narrow gauge from Alamosa to Durango was filed with the ICC on September 18, 1968. In July 1969, the ICC handed down the decision to abandon. Between the 1968 meeting and July 1969, a lot of support was needed in both states and elsewhere to save any portion of the narrow-gauge railroad.

There was much to be done.

CHAPTER 2

"SAVE THE NARROW GAUGE"

1968–1970

By the mid-1960s, the oil and gas industry development no longer required the large shipments of pipe and other equipment that had sustained the line over Cumbres Pass. In 1967, the D&RGW announced that there would be no more passenger specials, which had also brought some revenue and interest to the railroad. The D&RGW applied for abandonment in September 1968. Before that, however, voices were raised in both Colorado and New Mexico: "Save the Narrow Gauge!"

In late 1966 and into the next year, rumors and speculation surfaced concerning the railroad's fate. In Chama, Edmund E. Vigil Jr., a retired AT&SF telegrapher, was called into service by the D&RGW for emergency work due to heavy snows that winter. He and fellow D&RGW telegrapher Amos Cordova (later vice-president of the Durango & Silverton) worked to get the trains moving again. Then the D&RGW asked Vigil if he would move to Salida, Colorado, and continue. He said no, but during this short time with the Rio Grande, Vigil heard, possibly from Cordova, about the impending application by the D&RGW to abandon the entire narrow gauge from Alamosa to Durango and Silverton, Colorado, and Farmington, New Mexico. Vigil tried to rally support without much initial success. That same year, Terrence E. (Terry) Ross, then a Santa Fe architect and rail historian, saw carloads of new, narrow-gauge ties in the Alamosa yards. He was aware that the installation of those ties gave the railroad the necessary excuse of "rising costs being offset by declining revenues." This was further reason to apply to abandon the line.

At the same time in Colorado lived some folks who wanted to save the railroad. In Alamosa, the *Valley Courier* reported on October 15, 1968, that the "Colorado-New Mexico Citizens Group to Save the Railroad" had met. Attending were Pat Vigil, mayor of Antonito; Bud Nixon, of the Alamosa Chamber of Commerce; Floyd Kline of the Alamosa County Commission; Joe Casias of the Conejos County Commission; and Floyd Cross of Santa Fe. This was not the first of such meetings. Others had been held at Durango, Pagosa Springs, Chama and Farmington. The main subject of the October meeting was to try to maintain regular service on the line. Opinions varied wildly in several of such meetings as to keeping the line in regular service, saving all or part of the line for tourists or variations in between.

In New Mexico, there already existed an organization of loyal railroad fans and historians to serve as an umbrella agency for those wishing to speak with a united voice. The Railroad Club of New Mexico was organized in 1959 and began publishing a newsletter called the *New Mexico Railroader*. The April 1968 issue, under the headline "Save the Narrow Gauge," reported on a meeting in Santa Fe on March 28 to explore possibilities for doing just that. Terry Ross and Ed Gerlitz organized this meeting with representatives from Albuquerque, Taos, Santa Fe, Chama and elsewhere. At the meeting were various state officials, including a representative of the New Mexico Planning Office. At the time, the state was in the process of establishing a historic preservation program in response to the Federal Historic Preservation Act of 1966. Until then, historic preservation in New Mexico was scattered among various agencies and the private Historical Society of New Mexico. Only a month later, then governor David Cargo appointed a small committee to help write pending legislation, which was enacted by the legislature in 1970. That act established the Cultural Properties Review Committee within the planning office. But this historic preservation program would not play an active role with the railroad until 1974.

The main question before the informal meeting that March in Santa Fe was, as reported in the *Railroader*, to investigate "the feasibility of…state… operating…or getting some group to operate in the event…the petition to abandon is granted."* The discussion then revolved around the reported cost of purchase, estimated by the D&RGW to be $1,400,000, with the cost to scrap the line at $800,000. Indications were from the railroad that "it might part with [it] for practically nothing to a responsible party." There were also legal and financial "entanglements" to be considered involving questions of land ownership, "even if the rails are still there." Furthermore, the various counties of both states were due taxes, to say nothing of "vandalism and public liability." The state planning official opined, "One of the best possibilities of doing something to retain part of the line (and the chances of that are not very good) would be to operate the section from Chama to Dulce as a tourist attraction. This would be short enough that tourists would take the line to ride behind a steam engine!"

This discouraging bit of talk set the atmosphere for the remainder of the meeting. Other speakers urged folks to speak at ICC hearings against abandonment, due to the need for trains. Another said that there was not enough money for teachers much less than for a tourist railroad. He wondered whether the federal government working with various airlines might be able to attract foreign tourists. With that, the members then watched some movies by RR Club member Ernest Robart and adjourned.

In the meantime, the application by the D&RGW to the Interstate Commerce Commission proceeded. In April and May 1968, ICC hearings were held in Farmington, Durango and Alamosa. The upshot of these meetings was ICC examiner Robert Burchmore recommending abandonment, with an official ruling to come later.

In light of that recommendation, Terry Ross, Herman Barkmann, Warner Johnson and Larry Meyer "formed a Citizens Committee for Preservation of the Denver and Rio Grande Narrow Gauge Railway."[*] This group proposed that the line from Alamosa to Silverton "be made a national monument," which resulted in "several thousand signatures on a petition to the National Park Service." Of course, what the NPS would do was "uncertain" and might take five years. The problem was too urgent and immediate to wait that long.

Into the picture came Mr. Thomas Hinman. As far back as 1967, Hinman, once a reporter for the *Rocky Mountain News* in Denver, proposed to run a train from Alamosa. He was president of the Rio Grande & San Juan Railway Company, which owned several pieces of narrow-gauge rolling stock from Mexico. His proposal was to run a "new train" on the old track to re-create the San Juan Limited, one of the named passenger trains on the narrow gauge. The board of directors included, among others, Don Alfonso J. Miranda y Covarrubias of Mexico City. Hinman longed to create an atmosphere "reminiscent of this area's early cattle and mining days." Mr. Hinman's efforts, like so many others at the time, came to naught, except for his legacy of one coach still on the Cumbres & Toltec.

In 1968, meetings were continuing in an effort to "save the narrow gauge." Chaired by Eddie Vigil, a group of notables representing both states, the federal government and the D&RGW met to search for a federal grant in order to study private operation. Included were Santa Fe mayor Jardy Jones; Governor David F. Cargo of New Mexico; Lieutenant Governor E. Lee Francis, also of New Mexico; Robert McKinny, chairman of the President's Council on Travel; Alex McKinney, public relations director of the D&RGW; State Representative Ralph Gallegos; state senator Horace de Vargas; Colorado state representative Clarence Quinlan; and Jack Olsen, representative for Colorado governor John A. Love. Still others at the meeting included Marian Pearlman of the Four Corners group; Mike Valentine of the Santa Fe Chamber of Commerce; and William Riggs, representing the Jicarilla Apache tribe. All or most of these figures met in various towns affected by the threatened abandonment—Durango, Antonito, Alamosa and Farmington.

At one of these meetings, Carl Turner, general manager of New Mexico Rural Electrification Cooperative, asked the question, "Do you want to organize?" The answer was loudly affirmative. Turner proposed a board of directors of eleven members, one each from every town from Alamosa to Durango. The purpose was "the preservation of the D&RGW Narrow Gauge…Alamosa to Durango…for its historic and economic value in Northern New Mexico and Southern Colorado." Members of the board were Terry Moynihan, president of the Highway 64 Association, Taos; Kenneth Lively, Chama; Horace de Vargas, Rio Arriba; Art Isgar, La Plata County; Frank Lily White, Farmington; Cliff Hartman, Alamosa; Patrick Vigil, mayor of Antonito; Jim Colegrove, Santa Fe County; and the tribal chairmen of the Jicarilla and Southern Ute tribes. Officers were elected from the group: Terry Moynihan, president; Pat Vigil, vice-president; and Jim Colegrove, secretary. There was no treasurer. That remained for the next meeting, planned for Pagosa Springs, July 27. Things were moving along.

In New Mexico, much of the impetus for saving the narrow gauge came from the members of the Railroad Club of New Mexico. The club was established in 1959 with the general purpose of preserving, protecting, researching and publishing about railroads in the state, then and now. These ambitions were to be achieved through a newsletter, the *New Mexico Railroader.* Terrence Ross of Santa Fe and Ed Gerlitz, both of the club, arranged a general meeting in Santa Fe for March 28, 1968. Members came to "meet with public officials from Santa Fe and Chama." Also present for this informal meeting was Kurt Ziebarth of the state planning office. Ziebarth called for "investigating the feasibility of…[the] state…operating…or getting some group to operate [the railroad] in the event…[the] petition to abandon is granted." The idea was still around that somehow the ICC would not allow an end to service along the route. At one point this same year, club member Ernie Robart testified before the ICC hearing. The club members took more active roles in the fate of the narrow gauge.

At the Santa Fe meeting, Ziebarth said that the salvage value was $1,400,000, according to the D&RGW estimate, and that scrapping the line would cost $800,000, as noted before. "He [again] indicated that the D&RGW might part with [it] for practically nothing to a responsible party." He also saw legal and financial problems and noted that since the line crossed the state line, federal regulations would apply. Some of the land might revert to original owners even with the rails in place, and taxes were due to Rio Arriba and San Juan Counties in New Mexico to the amount of $28,000 per year, with larger amounts due to the Colorado counties. Finally, still throwing cold water, Ziebarth was sure that even a nonprofit operator would have to pay the taxes, to say nothing of "vandalism and public liability." That was when Mr. Ziebarth suggested a short run from Chama to Dulce, New Mexico, as a tourist attraction. "This would be short enough that tourists would take the line to ride behind a steam engine!" Not to be discouraged, Mike Valentine related the story of the fight in Durango to save the Silverton branch some nine years before. In 1954, trains were running only three times per week, but within a short time, the trains were running every day and ridership was climbing in many figures. Durango had found a pot of gold. Valentine was manager of the Durango Chamber of Commerce before moving to the same position in Santa Fe. He was also the secretary-treasurer of the Colorado–New Mexico Better Transportation Association. Valentine urged more cooperation among the interested parties in all the counties.

In 1968, Colorado state senator Hugh Fowler; his brother, Parker; and Eugene Hoffman founded another group called the Colorado Society for the Preservation of the Narrow Gauge. This group was incorporated in 1970. In 1972, the name was officially changed to the Colorado & New Mexico Society. (This group continued until about 1980.) He and Colorado representative Clarence Quinlan began to rally support there with public solicitations, as well as state money, to save the narrow gauge.

There were several more informal groups devoted to the railroad. One called the Narrow Gauge National Movement was at least a suggestion by several men. Terrence Ross tried to tie a Citizens Committee for Preservation of the Denver and Rio Grande Narrow Gauge Railway into a proposal to make the entire line a national monument. Several thousand signatures were on a petition to the National Park Service. He and others realized that this would be a lengthy process that could take several years. The question was what to do in the meantime because the abandonment proceedings were moving along.

D&GRW officials started formal abandonment hearings in Denver on September 18, 1967, with testimony. Citing the lack of business, track

The D&RGW turntable at Chama and locomotive #166 become a combined stage for photographing the railroad's crew. The coal chute is seen in the background.

conditions and competition from trucks, they asserted that the salvage value was $2,200,000, with the cost of salvage set at $800,000, or a net salvage estimated to be $1,393,000. The railroad official speaking was willing to talk about possible purchase by New Mexico and would be willing to train people to run a tourist train. A preliminary statement was entered by a representative of the New Mexico Better Transportation Association to the effect that the D&RGW failed to provide service and even downgraded that reduced level of service. In part, the statement read that the petition to abandon was "without precedent…few times in history that a railroad has abandoned…or sought to [abandon]… before filing their application." There were "many years of calculated and deliberate downgrading," and the claim of competition from trucks meant that the D&RGW was competing with its own trucking company.

From 1957 on, the D&RGW reduced freight service from daily to triweekly, semiweekly and then only as needed, weather permitting. For three years, 1965 through 1967, the line was closed from December to May. Rio Grande Motorway, a company subsidiary, took up the slack. The company reported that the total number of loaded narrow-gauge cars for 1965 was 1,806; in 1966, the figure dropped to 1,194 and in 1967 to a low of 759. Company representatives also criticized the New Mexico State Corporation Commission "brief of proceedings" as "garish" and "gaudy." They complained of colored paper of various hues as being "unprofessional and inflammatory," with illustrations that implied a "public be dammed" charge.

The railroad, the company representative asserted, was still carrying lumber and forest products, livestock, building materials and other raw materials, but since 1963, the railroad had claimed an annual deficit of $500,000. The end was near. In July 1968, the ICC permitted the D&RGW to abandon the narrow-gauge railroad with the exception of the Durango–Silverton branch—that segment was still making a profit with a tourist operation. When New Mexico still balked, the Chama–Dulce section continued to run, but for only a short time, as it made no economic sense. It, too, would be scrapped.

Even before the ICC decision, the public pressure to save all or a portion of the narrow gauge continued to build. In late 1968, the National Park Service sponsored running a train across the entire line. At one point, the park service also proposed that the line might be

The San Juan Express passenger train departs Cumbres station, Colorado, atop Cumbres Pass. The station was built in the 1880s. The original section house, car inspector's house and remains of the old snowshed remain on Cumbres Pass.

included in the National Park System as a Historic Landmark or as a National Monument. But all of this would take time, as much as five years, probably too much time to save the railroad. This proposal came to no avail, and the park service lost interest, saying that the project was too expensive and impractical. Growing pressure in both the two states' public and private sectors was offsetting that lack of federal interest. In early 1969, the New Mexico legislature passed a joint memorial asking the Colorado body to join in a study to investigate the possibilities of "joint operation" of the railroad as a "tourist attraction."

On April 4, 1969, New Mexico's Governor David Cargo signed House Bill 230, which created the New Mexico Railroad Authority and provided a means to acquire and operate the railroad. (The New Mexico bill was carried by freshman representative Jack Stahl.) The law defined a future operator as "any person, firm or corporation...for profit or any nonprofit" that was in sound financial position to meet all future obligations. The purpose of the act was to buy and operate "any railroad of historical and scenic importance in New Mexico." The words "living museum" also appeared in the act.

The Authority was composed of several ex-officio members, including the governor, the director of the revenue bureau, the state investment officer, the director of parks and recreation and the state engineer. There were also three public members to be appointed by the governor. The act specified quarterly meetings in Santa Fe or at other places and times as necessary. The Authority could employ people needed to carry out the provisions of the act and spend money to improve and operate "a state-owned railroad system," among other actions. It could also enter into contracts, receive grants and gifts, issue bonds and use public and private money that was collected "to plan and accomplish…the purpose of the Railroad Authority Act." As a final and totally *inadequate* measure, the legislature appropriated $100 for two fiscal years in order to carry out these provisions, according to the March–April 1969 *New Mexico Railroader* (vol. 11, no. 3).

During all this time, public pressure continued to build. In New Mexico, the first official Authority meeting was held on July 8, 1969, in Governor David Cargo's conference room in the state capitol. This meeting was the "First Organizational Meeting of the New Mexico Railroad Authority as authorized by the House Bill 230." The meeting attendees were ex-officio and public members—the former were Governor Cargo, State Engineer Steve Reynolds, Commissioner of Revenue Frank James, Sam Dillard of parks and recreation and State Investment Officer Robert C. Mead, and the latter were Terry Ross, Mark McMahon and Eddie Vigil. Others present were Jackson Clark of the Colorado Railroad Authority, Walter Bruce of Governor Love's office, Bill Krutch of parks and recreation and others. The first order of business was to agree to another meeting with Colorado Railroad Authorities in Chama on August 21. The main business was to adopt rules and regulations, policies and procedures, duties of the Authority and so forth—housekeeping, as it were.

All was not always so optimistic. The *Denver Post* reported at one point that New Mexico was still reluctant, even though there was "tentative agreement" between the D&RGW and the Authorities for a sale price of $588,900. More opposition appeared in the *Albuquerque Journal* written by columnist Eric McCrossen, referring to the proposed purchase as "Cargo-Love Choo-Choo Folly [the]…dog-gondest inter-state fiasco… since Black Jack Ketcham lost his head in Clayton." (Tom "Black Jack" Ketcham was a notorious bad man. Finally captured, he was sentenced to hang. During his time in jail, he gained a great deal of weight. So, when the trap was sprung, he was decapitated by the noose rather than having his neck broken.) McCrossen acknowledged the success of the Durango line but wondered why that success was not translated to the Cumbres line by the D&RGW "rather than unload it on" the two states. He quoted an unidentified railroader, probably John Norwood's article in the *Denver Post*, who criticized the project as "a Dinosaur."

McCrossen went on to quote Terry Ross, who said that the line was in good shape. "Further reports," noted McCrossen, about "that old Cargo-Love Choo-Choo Folly, await word from the cinderlands." In another column, McCrossen reported riding on the railroad in the *Albuquerque Journal* and how the volunteers and former railroad men impressed him. "It could indeed become a major tourist attraction," he suggested, but he wondered if the legislature would spend money "to operate the largest operating railroad museum in the nation." He admitted that a person should spend time with the volunteers "to become a believer."

A westbound freight train, pulled by a double-header, stops at Cumbres station, Colorado, in the 1940s.

Momentum continued to build. It being one year since the first Chama meeting, a second meeting adopted a new name: Better Transportation Group. A proposed $1,000 "feasibility" study was criticized and arguments rehashed the reasons for abandonment, but there was still hope for freight and tourist service. In April 1969, newspapers in the San Luis Valley, the *Valley Courier* and *Ledger-News* of Antonito, reported on the "unproductive meeting in Chama" and noted that the feasibility study was "completely negative." On the other hand, Representative Clarence Quinlan said that both legislatures were considering similar bills to purchase the line. Neither state could make a move, of course, until the respective legislatures met in the spring of the following year, 1970.

Many problems remained, with opinions for and against purchase being heard. For instance, Governor Cargo of New Mexico won the support of John Mershon, representative from Cloudcroft, with an alleged (by Governor Cargo) personal inspection trip to Chama. Mr. Mershon finally agreed to the project as they passed through the historic town of Abiquiu on the return trip from Chama. Former critic Eric McCrossen changed his mind but worried that "Little Railroad may not make All the Grades." He quoted Eddie Vigil to the effect that the railroad was the "key" to major recreational development in the region. McCrossen then went on (in "Rail Project Participation Makes Sense"): "I must admit…among those skeptics who questioned the sanity of both [states]…becoming involved in the [C&TS]…[as] unlikely parties that befuddles even the most optimistic recreation promoter." He added that "the longer you look [at a tourist operation] the better the railway looks." Critic William O'Donnell of Santa Fe, however, referred to the project as "a nuisance for future governors to be worried with…an absolute shambles of rotten wood and rusty metal."

By May 1970, however, the *Denver Post* was reporting a "tentative agreement" between the parties, although any proposed purchase of line from Chama to Durango, in addition to the Antonito–Chama segment, was refused by the D&RGW. On May 22, the *Albuquerque Tribune* reported that Colorado had appropriated the purchase money to match that previously approved by New Mexico, and in July that year, the two states bought the sixty-four miles of track, rolling stock, locomotives and tools from the D&RGW for the agreed $550,000. "The time for skepticism should be past," wrote "new believer" Eric McCrossen. On September

2, 1970, the *Valley Courier* reported that locomotive #483 made the first run on the new line.

Now the questions were very large. In the interim, between taking the check to Denver to pay the D&RGW (see the T. Ross article in *C&TS Dispatch*), there were volunteer excursions, the transfer of rolling stock by the D&RGW to Antonito and the volunteers getting it over to Chama for winter storage. There was also necessary preparation of the roadbed and rails for the 1971 season. Also, at that point in late 1970, there was no interstate agency to supervise. There was no railroad operator as yet, and the volunteers were determined to play a role, but that role was not yet defined. There was much to be done, including choosing a name for the new project. Terry Ross solved the matter by referring to the "highest point on the railroad, Cumbres Pass and the lowest, the bottom of Toltec Gorge"—hence the Cumbres & Toltec Scenic Railroad.

Throughout 1970, there was a confusion of voices, with various agencies, public and private, trying to arrive at a system for running the new historic railroad. The two states each had separate Railroad Authorities,

The San Juan passenger train is halted at Sublette, Colorado, and the crew and passengers mill about on the ground. The Sublette station is located on the line between the Toltec Gorge and Antonito, Colorado.

plus the Colorado and New Mexico Society for the Preservation of the Narrow Gauge Inc. and the Narrow Gauge Railroad Association Inc. were linked together through an Executive Committee. This confused situation was only further complicated by the addition of an independent contractor to operate the trains. Continuing into 1971, this confusion showed in the minutes of an Ad Hoc Committee on Joint Consensus, held in Chama on October 2, called by Chairman (pro-tem) Parker Fowler. Participants represented the Colorado & New Mexico Society for Preservation of the Narrow Gauge, the Narrow Gauge Association, members and officers. The principal order of business was "Inter-Association Relations," followed by "Communications between Society/Association and Railroad Authorities/Concessionaire." This would be a tall order, clearly illustrating the need for more formal arrangements.

The spring of l971 was momentous enough, with the two "sovereign" states having bought a tourist railroad, but as seen, the time had come for something to be done by legislative act, as well as other, more formal arrangements. In the Colorado legislature that spring, Representative Clarence Quinlan thought that something could be worked out for the 1972 sessions of each legislature. The two legislatures began some preliminary talks toward creating an Interstate Compact, but there were disagreements, all of which would delay any acts until 1972, as Mr. Quinlan had predicted. In the meantime, volunteers ran excursions, and the movie *Shoot Out* was filmed. In Chama, the first boxcar was converted for passenger use (riders then and now know the older red cars), and in Antonito, more volunteers were laying track, with three switches to create a turning wye. The historic junction at Antonito was not included in the purchase price, since those tracks were still being used by the D&RGW. Therefore, a new rail yard was planned on a five-acre plot to the west of the junction. This was on land donated by Mr. and Mrs. B.D. Griffin in September 1971. Storage space for fifty tons of spare parts and tools was located in garages and basements in the town.

New Mexico submitted a plan under the proposed compact to set up a private corporation, with five incorporators: two selected by each governor and a fifth to be elected by the four. The corporation would then lease the railroad from the proposed Authority. The only trouble was that such a plan was illegal in Colorado and, therefore, "rejected" by Colorado. In October 1971, Governor Bruce King of New Mexico

The San Juan stopped at Sublette. This photograph from the late 1910s depicts Sublette with picnickers, perhaps on a holiday. Sublette was an active stop at this time. The photograph was originally in the Joyce Collection.

wrote to Governor John A. Love of Colorado to say that he (King) had appointed Terry Ross to the New Mexico Railroad Authority to work on the Interstate Compact and that Eddie Vigil of Chama was to represent New Mexico on the joint Executive Committee of the Railroad Authority.

Back on August 1, 1971, Steve E. Reynolds, New Mexico state engineer, had written to Clarence Quinlan to report that "[o]n March 30, 1971, Governor Love appointed a committee of Coloradoans and by letter dated March 25, 1971, Governor King appointed a committee of New Mexicans to jointly draft an interstate compact for the operation of the Cumbres And Toltec Scenic Railway." How long it would take was a matter of conjecture; however, wrote King, "I suggest that we should soon take the first step to be sure that a product is available for consideration at the forthcoming sessions of our legislatures." King further proposed "that we use the compact approved by the 1971 session of the New Mexico legislature as a point of departure and that the committees meet in Santa Fe at 10:00 a.m. on September 23 to initiate discussions of appropriate changes in that version of a compact. A copy of the compact approved by the New Mexico legislature is attached."

Back in the summer of 1970, the two states had reached an accord in which they agreed "to purchase, preserve and maintain" a narrow-gauge railroad. Both bodies agreed also to receive title to the property, with each holding 50 percent ownership. Responsibility was also equally divided, with all legal actions requiring the approval of both bodies, such as cancellation clauses and so forth. Most urgently, perhaps, was the creation of an Executive Committee of four members, two from each state Authority. This committee was to organize itself with officers drawn from its own members and was granted specific powers "subject to the prior approval of each of the parties." Although given the power to "employ necessary officers," the committee was to "designate" whether such agent was an employee of the Colorado Railroad Authority or of the New Mexico Railroad Authority. That agent was then subject to the constitution and laws of whichever Authority was applicable. This agreement attempted to split that agent between the two states by specifying which Authority employed him, depending on where in each state the agent spent the majority of his time. If the time was spent equally in each state, then the question of his employer was left up the two Authorities to decide. This agreement would create more confusion. There were other housekeeping matters taken care of, and the agreement was then signed by Governors Love on June 30 and Cargo in July 1970, respectively.

That agreement was not the end because, as events demonstrated, more legislative action was required. Then, in early 1971, the New Mexico legislature acted. "An Act Relating to Railroads" was passed, providing a bi-state compact to establish the means for operation of the C&TSRR. There also was language "encouraging…recreation, and preservation of a 'living' museum." The compact further provided for a leasing arrangement with an operator that would be responsible for rehabilitation, improvement and maintenance. There was a provision for an annual rental, which depended on "net distributable profits after taxes." There was also a clause allowing termination of the lease if the operator suffered "insolvency, bankruptcy or dissolution." The real point, in this idea from New Mexico, was to create an operating corporation that would lease the railroad from the states under this compact. The existing Railroad Authorities did not affect the Authority, or its powers "except as provided in this article [9]." That was true only if compatible

Locomotive #482 is shown stopped at Sublette, Colorado, on January 8, 1949, in this photograph by Robert W. Richardson. The San Juan Mountains of the Rockies, through which the line runs, have recorded individual storms with snowfalls of five feet or more.

with this compact. Otherwise, all previous agreements between the states were "terminated."

Section 3 of the compact provided that, upon the effective date of this compact, the New Mexico Railroad Authority should enter into a lease with the railroad corporation "to be formed in accordance with the compact." And the lease should comply with the provisions of Section 1 of this act. This proposal from New Mexico did not sit well, however, with Colorado. There were differing philosophies as to how to govern this joint railroad project. Negotiations between representatives of both states continued on into 1972.

There were those in Colorado back in 1970 who accused New Mexico of dragging its feet on the purchase, and now, early in 1972, "T. Ross [was] the continuing fly in the soup." The source of some of the friction between the states was summed up in a memorandum from J. Kenneth Green, secretary of the Colorado Railroad Authority, to the members of the New Mexico Authority. "At times," he wrote, "activities have been made more awkward because of differences in operating philosophies in the two states." The New Mexico Railroad Authority takes "a very active part in the day to day operations and negotiations," whereas in Colorado "the Executive Committee members have been given more latitude than in New Mexico." Green pointed out the obvious: "[T]his has caused some confusion…as to just who is the boss at any given time." This confusion mentioned in the Green memorandum pointed to larger issues, even larger than those of different "philosophies." While this search for an interstate agreement on governing the railroad continued, in 1971 there was the need to select an operator. Also in the wings was the volunteer Narrow Gauge Railroad Association (NGRRA), looking for a role to play. By July 1972, the two states had agreed on a compact linking the two Authorities through a Joint Executive Committee. It was hoped that the hurdle was now surmounted and that the governing bodies could get to work. Events would prove such an assumption to be wrong.

CHAPTER 3

OPERATOR AND
VOLUNTEERS

While the two Railroad Authorities struggled to reach agreement, a national search for an operator was launched at the same time. Volunteers were also at work preparing for operations by working on track, altering boxcars to passenger coaches and the like. Volunteers also ran several trips on the line to bring rolling stock across to Chama before shutting down for the winter. The two states owned an "operating" railroad.

In the early fall of 1971, the Authorities placed two advertisements, September 16 and 21, in the *Wall Street Journal* for an operator. The ads listed the general numbers of rolling stock, nine steam locomotives, "supporting structures" and a gross income of about $100,000 for thirty-eight days of operations. Future operations called for an "eventual minimum" of one hundred days, with a profit to come out of gross revenues. Any lessee was to have enough capital for "rehabilitation and maintenance" and would develop recreational and tourist facilities. There was also an article in the *National Observer* on October 2, 1971. The *Journal* ads produced about fifty answers, while the *Observer* resulted in some seventy-five inquiries. These requirements were probably too optimistic considering the age of the equipment and track.

Some of these replies were quite serious, from other operating railroads and rail fan groups, for instance. Other inquires, on the other hand, were very frivolous, being written on hotel stationery, casual notepaper or even a telegram. Also represented in the inquiries were land developers and real estate agents—hardly railroad operators and clearly with agendas other than historic preservation. There was one notable offer from a firm that was "well financed and has the personnel…to develop this project." But it also wanted a ninety-nine-year lease, an impossible request. A second serious contender for the contract was called the Toltec Corporation. This group was headed by two individuals from Chicago. Their application came months after the September deadline. When asked at the February 1972 meeting why they had missed the deadline, the Toltec representatives replied that the needed financing was not in place at the time of the deadline. They continued looking for necessary financing and still hoped to participate. Since at that moment no contract had been signed, the Toltec proposal was placed before the Authorities. After reading the Toltec proposal, Jackson Clark moved to set aside the proposal and to proceed on with the agenda and Scenic Railway's proposal. In subsequent discussions, the Toltec Corporation was noted as not as capable as Scenic.

From all of these interested parties, whimsical or not, emerged one company with railroad experience and with demonstrated financial resources. In the latter matter, Scenic president Robert Keller submitted a report from Dun & Bradstreet dated April 22, 1971. This report noted that the company was incorporated in June 1970 with "authorized" capital of $500,000, paid in capital (cash) of $210,000 as of April 22, 1971. The report covered operations, revenue and expenses of Scenic Railways Corporation while operating a tourist railroad at South Lake Tahoe on leased land. The train operated from July 4, 1970, to September 5, 1970. Total sales were $13,600. Officers of the company were Robert Keller, president; John Houghton Jr., vice-president; John Allan Jr., vice-president; Melvin L. Hawley, secretary; and Ralph W. Kane, treasurer. The directors were David B. Ogle, Eugene L. Watson and William Earl Bell, chairman.

Scenic directors and officers bought shares of stock in the company at $10 per share for a total of $60,000. The corporation had borrowed $25,000 from Directors Earl Bell and Eugene Watson. The report noted also that Keller expected to sign another contract shortly for another railway site in the West: "That railroad (C&TS) should operate this summer (1971)." The report also noted that the "[c]urrent condition (of Scenic) [is] undetermined. Trade slowness is reported and there

The San Juan is stopped in 1915 at Garfield Monument so that passengers can inspect the memorial. The structure, near Rock Tunnel, was erected by members of the National Association of General Passenger and Ticket Agents who held a memorial burial service on this spot on September 26, 1881, for U.S. president James A. Garfield, who died on September 19 of infection and complications caused by an assassin's bullet.

appears to be a restricted cash position. Net worth is placed at $136,000 after exclusion of intangible assets. Trend is up. Sales for 1970 were $13,600 and are projected at $60,000 for 1971." By comparison to other applicants, Scenic appeared to be the best.

Scenic Railways Inc., a California corporation, had a railroad at Lake Tahoe, some rolling stock, locomotives and track. Scenic learned of the need for a C&TS operator from the *Iron Horse News*, the newsletter of the Colorado Railroad Museum at Golden, Colorado. Subsequently, Scenic was awarded the contract, on February 23, 1972. Scenic had incorporated on May 20, 1970, and by-laws were adopted on June 28 that year. Scenic had a short-term agreement to operate C&TS trains for the remainder of 1971 and had also agreed to do considerable work on locomotives, conversion of cars and track upgrade. On September 13, 1971, Scenic submitted to the Authorities a "Final Invoice" of $38,448.51 as a final payment of a total of $73,700.54 for work done that year.

Three more actions were taken at this most important meeting. Vice-chairman Terry Ross raised the question of hiring an agent to represent the Authorities in the actual operations of the train. They decided that such an individual ought to be a "management type." Mr. Quinlan believed that this agent should have some mechanical abilities also. A salary of $15,000 to $20,000 was deemed reasonable. Virgil Bockhaus had done this job up to the moment. The hiring of such an agent was left up to the Joint Executive Committee. All members also noted that the agent "must take an interest and help Scenic make good." That was the obligation of the Authorities to the states.

Finally, while the contract with Scenic still required approval from both attorneys general, Scenic needed to get to work immediately. The Joint Authorities instructed the Executive Committee to "prepare a letter to Scenic allowing them to go on the premises and begin preparing the train for the oncoming season, as long as no liability is incurred by either State." This was made as a motion and passed without dissent. Along with the formal paperwork, the committee members asked Keller for books and records of the 1971 summer operation. Also, the Joint Executive Committee was informed of the matter of the burned lava water tank and the possibility of replacing it with the unused tank at Antonito. For the cost of about $5,000, the replacement would work.

After Scenic was awarded a twenty-year operating contract, much more was left to be done before operations could begin in 1972. More boxcars were converted, Scenic brought a small forty-four-ton diesel locomotive from the defunct Oahu Railroad in Hawaii to the property, the volunteers painted and stenciled rolling stock and there were special runs: a moonlight train to Osier for dinner and the Santa Fe Opera Guild benefit train for that famous company.

In the meantime, the original volunteers' group was in administrative limbo. It had no real standing either with the Authorities or with Scenic. Something had to be done or a valuable resource and active and committed volunteers would be lost. Legislative grants for both operations and historic preservation and repair of the many historic pieces simply were not forthcoming. Only grudgingly did the two legislatures provide enough money, usually $10,000 each per year, to operate a small office for the Authorities, so a continuing support element, such as the volunteers, was quite essential.

In April 1971, one group of interested volunteers organized and called itself the "Volunteer Board of Operating Supervisors…[with the purpose] to aid in organizing and coordinating volunteer efforts" on the railroad. Most of these folks were involved in the movement of equipment by rail from Antonito to Chama in 1970. That experience convinced many of those individualistic volunteers that the lack of an organization would jeopardize safety and that their organization could be helpful to "future interest" of the railroad. They also needed to be recognized by both the Authorities and the operator. As of April 20, 1971, the process for incorporating an organization was underway.

The Narrow Gauge Railroad Association was being incorporated in New Mexico as a nonprofit, tax-exempt corporation and with membership open to the public. It would be a charitable, educational association: the "purpose of this corporation is to aid in the ultimate preservation, restoration, display, and operation of narrow gauge railroad equipment… for public use and enjoyment." This New Mexico corporation was to be filed as a foreign corporation in Colorado. This organization would act on any level of activity to benefit the railroad. This activity could cover anything from rebuilding track to operating trains, procuring and restoring additional narrow-gauge equipment, serving as curator of "a narrow gauge museum" and subcontracting its services to the operator. This group already represented "dedicated, interested, and…knowledgeable narrow gauge railroad fans." There were several experienced railroad men, both active in and retired from operating railroads. Safety engineers and insurance underwriters were also represented: "We remain ready to serve, and would be happy to furnish further information on our organization. We hope the Authority will find us of some assistance." The letter announcing this program was signed by President Alan Stevens and sent to members of both Authorities.

The week before, on April 14, Stevens sent Terry Ross a preliminary letter explaining in much the same words the aims and purposes of this new organization. Back in the fall of 1970, Stevens, Ken Pruitt, Allen Stevenson and Alan Stevens prepared to organize a volunteer group. This was done with Terry Ross's prior knowledge and support. What Stevens proposed was about twelve "foremen or supervisors," each being charged with specific areas, such as coordinating work, safety, work priorities, procurement of materials, work crews and so forth. Each supervisor would be responsible for safety rules, tool and equipment security and good communications with the operator, Authorities and so on.

Stevens hoped that each supervisor would be given specific areas of responsibility by the Railroad Authorities, perhaps in written form. In turn, the organization would provide written instructions, rules, order forms, tool and equipment forms and so on. "We hope," he wrote, "this proposal will meet the approval of the…Authority, to better provide for the ultimate success of the railroad." Stevens included a list of prominent individuals and their projected responsibilities. This list read like a who's who of committed rail fans: Ken Pruitt, Allen L. Stevenson, Dick Glass, Ernest W. Robart, Al Chione, John Pritchard, Virgil Bockhaus, Mike Carr, Alan Stevens and Dan Pyzel—almost all of the New Mexico supporters. Colorado was to be represented by Joe "Swede" Johnson of Antonito.

That summer, 1971, the NGRRA began to publish a newsletter, the *Narrow Gauge Railroad-News*. This was in cooperation with the older Railroad Club of New Mexico. It published two issues before spinning off its own newsletter, the *Telltale*. In that first issue, July–August 1971, was the announcement that the new organization was designated to be responsible for all volunteer labor on the C&TS for the rest of that year. In exchange for the promise of insurance coverage for its members, the NGRRA promised to provide five "Car Attendants" for each weekend run and for the weekday runs when possible. The attendants would ride free and, in return for the ride, handle the folding steps and car windows and answer questions from the passengers. The old car body bunkhouse in Chama was for the use of the volunteers. Member Russell Smith was in charge of volunteers' schedules.

By August 3, the *Albuquerque Tribune*, under the headline "Off the Beaten Path" by veteran newsman Howard Bryan, quoted president Alan Stevens that membership in the NGRRA was up to 140. A general meeting of the NGRRA was held in Albuquerque on August 30. Members of the board of directors were named: Allen L. Stevenson, Dan Pyzel, Richard A. Glass, Ernest W. Robart, Russell F. Smith, Al Chione, Joe C. Johnson, John Oldberg and Larry Broadway. Scenic president Robert Keller reported activities in Chama, and Joe (Swede) Johnson did the same for Antonito.

In the September–October 1971 issue of *Narrow Gauge Railroad-News* was a report of the last trains on October 9–11. In the previous issue,

Robert Keller had reported that locomotive #484 was ready to operate, having passed inspection. Over the winter, carpenters and volunteers converted a dozen boxcars to passenger cars. This was all ready for the June 26, 1972 inaugural run. There were 150 people on a trip from Chama to Antonito sponsored by the New Mexico Railroad Club. On Sunday, June 27, another VIP special ran with another 150 persons on board. There were run-bys for photographers and a picnic lunch at Osier. From then on, for the remainder of that 1972 season, trains ran 90 percent full on average. Trains ran on weekends, with one round trip on weekdays. Passengers were bused from Antonito to Chama. There was a special on October 2 for the Society of Professional Geologists. This resulted in a book published by the geologists of New Mexico State Bureau of Mines. The 1972 operating season ended on a positive note, but there was much yet to be done.

As noted earlier, a permanent operator had been signed to a twenty-year contract, a working relationship between the Authorities of each state and the operator was beginning to be clarified and all these matters were moving along with the volunteers anxiously awaiting their ambiguous role to be more clearly defined. There was still a lot of immediate work to do on the railroad, its track, equipment, buildings and preparations for the coming years. The volunteer groups were equally in need of closer cooperation.

LEGAL MATTERS, 1971 AND 1972

In the autumn, the future looked a bit more secure what with an operator under contract with the governing bodies and the volunteers helping to provide a third important element. However, there were still some housekeeping matters to be done before things might go a little more smoothly. Starting back in 1970, there was a string of requests to the New Mexico attorney general's office regarding a variety of legal questions associated with many subjects—starting with the negotiations to buy the railroad in the first place. That first memorandum to Governor Cargo covered details of New Mexico's legal right to take title by quitclaim deed. That particular memorandum left open the questions of title to right-of-way and to water rights. The D&RGW did not rule out the purchase of

An extremely long mixed-freight train travels eastbound at the Los Pinos turn in Colorado. This train carries lumber and oil and pulls boxcars as well as other cars.

the historic depot at Antonito but pointed out the obvious problem of the distance of half a mile from that building to the beginning of narrow-gauge track. New Mexico's attorney general Mark B. Thompson III said that merely accepting the deeds and bill of sale and paying the purchase price could constitute the whole purchase. This was only beginning to settle these legal matters.

On into 1971, there was a flurry of letters and opinions. Questions of insurance protection for both an operator and the Authorities were raised and ultimately answered with proof of such presented. Public records were to be open to all, excluding medical histories of those involved for reasons of privacy. Certification from the Interstate Commerce Commission was required, but for a while, there was confusion as to who should get it—the Authorities or the operator. Finally, the operator received the certificate. Perhaps one of the sillier, but typical, matters was the question of the newly hired Dan Pyzel's title. In a letter, the New Mexico attorney general, in addressing several matters of procedure, decided that Pyzel's title as "Official Secretary" to the Authority would better be "Executive Secretary." Ultimately, his title was that of "Consultant."

Through the fall and winter of 1971–72, plans were laid for the first real season with Scenic Railway operating the railroad, the Authorities and the Executive Committee overseeing and Scenic and a volunteer group helping. Scenic's 1972 schedule showed the essential operation of four consecutive days, being one-way trips to or from Chama or Antonito. "Motor coaches" provided transportation to either destination and/or return to the original starting point. The rider could begin the trip at either Chama or Antonito, and the bus trip was either before or after the train ride. Serious road and track work began in April 1972 to prepare for operations. Executive Secretary Dan Pyzel reported on activities starting the week of April 24. Track foreman Bobby Sanchez inspected the line and then put a full crew of section hands to work clearing mudslides near Mud Tunnel (Tunnel No. 1). Locomotive #484 was made ready by the twenty-seventh and steamed up. All was ready for a "run-through" to Antonito to pick up some rolling stock purchased by Scenic.

The train was also to pick up the Hinman coach and a Railroad Post Office car for use by a movie company (the movie *Showdown* was being

Engine #479, pulling the westbound D&RGW San Juan passenger train, takes on water in Antonito, Colorado, before ascending toward Cumbres Pass. This photograph was taken on July 14, 1947, by Dan Howe.

filmed). Jim Schaucroft, an experienced D&RGW engineer and the main engineer for Scenic this season, was at the controls of #484. Veteran locomotive engineer Ben Greathouse supervised him. Greathouse, incidentally, offered the opinion that the track was in as good a shape as he had ever seen it—with the exception of the area of the "narrows." The "narrows" are so named for that location just north of Chama where the highway and railroad right-of-way are squeezed between the mountain on one side and the Chama River Canyon on the other. The Chama–Antonito trip was uneventful, save for one large rock on the tracks, which was rolled out of the way. The train remained in Antonito for that night.

The next morning, Friday, April 28, 1972, the train was delayed when a front loader to refuel #484 did not arrive. While waiting, Pyzel and Clarence Quinlan inspected the reroofing of the lava tank pump house by Swede Johnson, deep in the canyon of the Rio de Los Pinos. Water from the river used to be pumped from there to the lava tank high on the mesa above. Although no longer used, the pump house is a reminder of railroad-related construction of the last century. Built of hand-cut lava in 1883, it was connected by 2,230 feet of three-inch iron pipe to the lava water tank, which sits about 600 feet above the river. It served well into the 1960s. The train trip back to Chama was uneventful. That same afternoon, a meeting between Scenic and Authority members took place to clear up some details of the final lease, which was done shortly.

The final accomplishment before the season could start was the paving of New Mexico Highway 17 through the "narrows." Highway widening and paving had partially blocked the rail line through the "narrows," which volunteers and the contracting company had repaired in 1971. The loose materials from that construction continued to slide down onto the track, even trapping a work train on one occasion. The result was a contract between the New Mexico Highway Department and Universal Constructors of Albuquerque to pave the road and construct a retaining wall along the railroad in the "narrows." The paving was done in the summer, and after the 1972 season, the wall was built. There was a total of 2,300 feet of wall, in three sections, consisting of steel sections held in place by columns every ten to fifteen feet. Rails and ties were removed, the walls constructed and backfilled, the railroad grade and drainage ditches reconstructed and the relaying of the rail and ties achieved. All

A passenger train is about to depart from the Antonito, Colorado depot on August 30, 1941, in this photograph taken by John W. Maxwell.

of this planning was done on May 23, and the work was done later. The cost was about the same money as the two states paid for the railroad in the first place.

Everything was almost ready. There were still some boxcars to convert into passenger cars, and then the season could begin. All seemed in place: the operator Scenic, the Authorities and the Volunteers—along with their own newsletter, the *Telltale*. At the same time, Antonito celebrated the return of the very historic locomotive #463 as a gift to the town of Antonito from its former owner, famous movie cowboy Gene Autry. Built in 1903, it was the oldest locomotive on the C&TS Railroad. Hopes were high to both display and operate this historic locomotive. The dream of operation was far into the future.

Narrow Gauge Railroad Association volunteers were serving as car attendants by coordinating their efforts with Scenic management, with attendants scheduled for all days of operations. The volunteers were also trying to get other aspects of their organization in place. There was every indication of a systematic approach to the many problems of starting up the tourist season. Car attendants were only one such problem. Members were offered a course in first aid, and within a short time, twenty-one members were qualified. A Public Information Committee was created to handle the newsletter, press and other releases for public and media and memos on internal matters, such as meeting notices. All of these items were meant to provide consistent and accurate information to the public. Also, the volunteers soon began a program of restoration of historic buildings and rolling stock.

Their first project was the Rotary OM and its tender for a display atop Cumbres Pass. As with all of the rolling stock that was stored in the open, weather had taken a heavy toll on Snowplow OM. Lack of maintenance in the last years of D&RGW operations and more recent vandalism had left the historic OM with a leaking roof, broken windows, peeling paint and rotten wood. Work was slow because of small work crews. This and other preservation/restoration work was projected to provide a complete snow fighting display at Cumbres for the summer season, with a locomotive, the Rotary OM, its water car, a bunk car and a flanger composing the exhibit.

A second project was the display of a typical freight train in the Chama yards. All of this work, real and unrealized, was done with the knowledge and approval of Scenic management and accompanied with emphasis on safety—hats, shoes, gloves, safety glasses and safety rules. In August 1972, NGRRA president Alan Stevens reported that there were a total of 140 members of the association. One month later, he reported a remarkable increase in the number of members to 250. Most of these volunteers were serving as car attendants, which was their primary obligation. President Stevens urged the members to participate in historic preservation projects. That June 26, the president of the Railroad Club of New Mexico, Ernest Robart, rode the first train. By the following October 24, at the end of the operating season, a reported 19,350 people had ridden that first full season.

The Narrow Gauge Railroad Association was growing, with activities all across the line, such as painting mileposts and lettering rolling stock and locomotives. The board of directors also started a program of creating local chapters. Increases in membership meant a larger geographical distribution. Cities such as Denver, Los Alamos, El Paso and others needed to have coordination with headquarters in Albuquerque. Emblems, plates and jackets embossed with the association emblem were placed on sale. The association had jointly sponsored with Scenic Railways a freight train and excursion train across the line.

A mixed-freight train, including tank cars, chugs up the grade from Los Pinos toward Cumbres station in this photograph taken by John Krause.

The newsletter also reported that a total of seventeen boxcars were converted for passenger cars. These were the final reports for both the operator and the volunteers for 1972. All in all, things looked very good for the coming season in 1973. Trouble, however, was on the way for both Scenic and the volunteers.

CHAPTER 4

FATAL YEARS

The Arab Oil Embargo and Volunteer Trouble

Problems began for the volunteers in late 1972. The last newsletter for the volunteers was in November, and another was not sent out until April 1973, with an apology from President F. Alan Stevens. The resignation of the editor delayed the newsletter, and members were too busy with new publications, such as a handbook and mile-by-mile guide, to put out another letter. It was hoped that a new board of directors, new officers and a new editor would increase communications with members about activities of both the association and the operations planned for 1973. In that regard, Scenic was also working on two more locomotives, with the expectation of having four operable for the season. Another optimistic note came in March 1973 when the C&TS was listed on the National Register of Historic Places—an honorary nomination that brought it under the protection of federal and state historic preservation programs.

A second and vastly more serious problem for Scenic also came in 1972 when the oil-producing Arab states raised the price of oil. Then, in 1973, as a result of U.S. support for Israel in the Yom Kippur War, the Arab states stopped shipments of oil to the United States altogether. This produced a major disruption of the western economies. It was particularly hard on the tourist industry and projects such as the Cumbres & Toltec.

All of that trouble was in the future, as in the spring of 1972, very optimistic plans were well along for the new season. For instance, heavy snowpack on Cumbres Pass required a special train to clear the snow

C&TSRR locomotives #463 and #497 pull away from the camera with freight on a curve below the spot known as Cresco, Colorado.

away. Early efforts used bulldozers to clear some of the track between Cresco and Los Pinos siding, but the snow had drifted in again. A flanger train, with locomotive #484 and a snowplow pilot; a flanger, locomotive #483; a flat car with a bulldozer; boxcar with tools and supplies; a crew car; and the historic caboose #0503 departed Chama early on May 12. The train left Chama but on reaching Cresco, the snow was piled up above the headlight on #484. This train was almost at the top when lead locomotive #484 and the trailing flanger derailed due to snow and ice that had drifted into a cut. The flanger was rerailed, but #484 wasn't until late the following day, May 13. From then on, things went well enough, and the whole operation was over by May 17. All was ready for the first regular train on May 25, 1972.

Meantime, the NGRR Association was contemplating bringing some more order to its own house. In the June newsletter, the treasurer reported on efforts to become a tax-exempt operation, an IRS 501(c)(3) organization. The problem was the high cost, with legal fees ranging from $500.00 to $1,000.00. This was deemed too much for the current budget, what with there being $1,285.37 on hand this June, so the call went out for a volunteer lawyer—with no apparent results. Also, a meeting was held between Scenic management and association leaders to prepare for operations for the coming season. Scenic's Bob Keller, Fritz Bauer, Gene Watson and John Oldberg praised the car attendant program as having a good effect on passengers. They hoped that the association would continue to support Scenic in this way. Preservation projects for the volunteers were also discussed. These included preparing a display train at Antonito, possibly repairing the snowshed at Cumbres, reroofing the historic caboose #0503 and milepost painting—a project begun the previous year.

During these discussions, one problem did emerge that was seemingly slight at the time. An association member had arrived in Chama on a long vacation trip and wanted to serve as a car attendant. This posed a problem because the car attendant program leadership was centered in Los Alamos and Albuquerque. Further, Scenic's employees were not aware of the details of the association's plans and resented taking time off from essential work to help the visitor find volunteer work. "Sometimes one hasty word leads to another" and "ill feelings are generated," leaving a bad taste in everyone's mouth. President Stevens went on to lament the incident and apologized for the lack of a solution.

Stevens continued with other news about current operations. Scenic's ticket sales were above the previous year. Trains were currently made up of eleven passenger cars. The possibility of twenty-car trains raised the question of double-heading, or running in two sections. A high side gondola as an open car at the end of the train was another experiment. This appeared to be very popular.

Stevens also announced the new car attendant rules and regulations. The attendant had to be a member of the NGRRA. Those wanting to serve had to contact the chief car attendant two weeks beforehand. Such requests were to be acknowledged by mail on a first-come, first-serve basis. Casual members arriving unexpectedly could be accepted only on a standby basis. There was one attendant for every two cars. They were directed to arrive at the depot one hour before departure. Those arriving only thirty minutes before departure would be considered as standby. Attendants had to be familiar with safety rules and have a good command of the history of the railroad from D&RGW times to the present C&TSRR. They also were advised to wear dark jeans, a NGRRA jacket and an engineer hat with a C&TS patch.

In Chama, volunteers were to park near and register at the bunkhouse. Antonito attendants rode busses there from Chama and assembled in the yard. Before departure, each attendant was to report to the chief of attendants, receive any special instructions and a car assignment and draw and sign for jacket, badge and information book. They were to understand operations and schedule, know whistle signals and safety rules and be assigned positions. The on-train duties included raising and lowering steps (boxcar conversions included steps cut into the midsection of each car that were drawn up to the side of the car). Volunteers were required to take a first-aid course. Such course being offered on July 14 and 15, 1973, meant that those passing the course received Red Cross cards. The car attendant was urged to report complaints, compliments, potential hazards or other problems. Lastly, the attendant was exhorted to remember that the passengers came *first*. All was in readiness and all looked forward to the coming season, but there was trouble looming on the horizon.

In other business that June, a new board of directors was elected: Al Chione and Larry Broadway from Denver, John Oldberg of Chama, Bill Luxford of Bernalillo, John Pritchard and Ike Miessner of Los Alamos and Jack La Munyon, Russ Smith, Phil Dater, Ernie Robart, Bill Moyers, Alan Stevens, Bill Wood and Ken Pruitt of Albuquerque.

On June 1, 1973, the new season began with locomotives #483 and #484 doing the work. For the first eighteen days, the trains carried an average of 213 passengers every operating day. There was a high of 365 and a low of 75. This was above the figures for 1972, despite the continuing gas "shortage." At least 43 volunteers rode as car attendants. Some painting was done in Chama, such as switch stands and part of the water tank, and a prime coat was applied to the bunkhouse door and one window.

Two members, June and Jim Demlow, bought the Chama Station Lodge (now the Chama Station Inn) and offered discounts on showers (twenty-five cents with your own soap and towel, fifty cents with motel supplies) plus a 10 percent discount on rooms, 50 percent if rooms were still available after 8:00 p.m. Demlow was employed in the business office of the New Mexico Institute of Mining and Technology in Socorro, New Mexico. John Pritchard was appointed by the governor to fill a vacancy on the New Mexico Railroad Authority. To prevent conflict of interest, Pritchard resigned from the NGRRA Board.

One of the early excursion trains of the Cumbres & Toltec Scenic Railroad is pulled by locomotive #484. These boxcars were modified for passenger transport. The location is on Tanglefoot Curve, east of Cumbres station.

Demlow was chairman of the Chama Bicentennial Committee. He embarked on an ambitious plan for that national celebration of the nation's birth. Principal among several projects was a plan for a railroad museum. He hoped that the NGRRA would manage the museum. The proposal was taken under consideration by board member Ken Pruitt. Then Jack LaMunyon resigned from the NGRRA Board and was replaced by Jim Demlow. Jim Case of Los Alamos was elected to fill another opening. The board was meeting the first Thursday of every month. The newsletter *Telltale* was then scheduled to appear after each meeting. This proved to be a very optimistic schedule. There were big gaps between issues—September to January for instance.

Scenic's management of the railroad continued to earn high marks with NGRRA members and other rail fans. Special runs with units of historic rolling stock augmented the regular trains on operating days. Pointedly, the editor of *Telltale* noted that rumors of cancelled runs were not true. The operator did have some late trains, but none was cancelled. In January 1974, Scenic operated the historic Rotary Snowplow OM as

The C&TSRR's engines #483 and #484 await departure of the daily excursion train out of the Chama depot.

a special attraction, hoping to raise a little revenue. In February, a much-expanded *Telltale* reported on the snowplow trip, including a photograph of the event. *Telltale* also carried a new logo and header (a head-on view of a locomotive). Rotary OM was put into operating condition by the cooperation of both volunteers and Scenic's own crewmembers, who volunteered to help. The former worked on the outside, including reroofing, while Scenic's people did the mechanical work. There were riders in an open gondola car, but many followed along on the highway; in the past, the road was seldom plowed, so the train operated alone. All in all, the NGRRA newsletter reported a great success.

In the meantime, the two state legislatures prepared to appropriate $100,000 each for the railroad. The money would be used for repairs to water tanks and other water systems work on the engine house and depot in Chama plus other bridge, trestle and track work. This was always a difficult matter. The process required that both states appropriate money in exactly equal amounts. Over the years of state ownership, there were several incidents when the time to get both legislatures to act took two or three years. Fortunately, both states agreed to hold such funds while waiting for the other to act. Scenic also tried to raise more funds by offering stock in the company. The price was five dollars per share, with a minimum of one hundred shares. This was not a great success.

As noted previously, financial troubles were compounded by the action resulting from the Yom Kippur War and the subsequent oil shortage. The oil-producing nations (OPEC for short) cut off the flow of Middle Eastern oil. This was the second time that OPEC had either raised the price of oil or actually stopped shipping oil. Oil-dependent western nations were thrown into economic chaos, bringing about profound effects on the tourist industry in the United States.

That spring, Scenic management regarded the long lines of cars at gas stations and "Out of Gas" signs as likely to have a negative effect on its revenues for the coming 1974 season. Therefore, it announced a new schedule, reducing the number of trains in 1974. It also announced that no steam trains would be run for the first part of the season, from May 25 through August 1. Instead, the ex–Oahu Railway diesel would operate from the top of Cumbres Pass to the ghost town of Sublette and return. These trips were on a four-days-per-week schedule: Saturday, Sunday, Tuesday and Thursday. Then the plan was to return to steam operations by August 3 until operations ceased on October 6. This plan meant that there would be only twenty steam trains in 1974. If the demand for more trains was enough to warrant them, more trains would be added. The use of the diesel, however, soon led to vocal criticism appearing in the press, as well as letters directed to Scenic management. This did not bode well for the future.

Scenic came in for other criticisms also. In July 1973, Scenic began work on the historic section house and depot at Osier, Colorado. Osier was the current lunch stop for the C&TS trains coming from both Chama and Antonito. Osier was once a small village on the toll road from Conejos to Chama. The section house and depot, water tank, coal loading dock, a small rooming house and stock yards all made up a typical stop on the railroad. It is located at an elevation of more than nine thousand feet above sea level, above the timberline, in open slopes that had once been heavily forested. A fire had burned the forest in the early 1870s before the railroad was built in 1880.

In a letter to the Authorities, Consultant Dan Pyzel noted the work being done on the historic buildings at Osier. The work on the

The eastbound San Juan passenger train travels past the Los Pinos water tank on September 16, 1948, in this photograph by Robert W. Richardson.

section house and depot was meant to accommodate the passengers for a lunch stop before the return trip. The depot was converted into restrooms, a process that did not have much effect on the outward appearance of the little historic building. Alterations to the section house were a different matter. That structure was not nearly big enough to serve passengers on both trains. Passengers would have to eat at picnic tables in the open. So Scenic decided to install a kitchen inside and build a shed roof over the food service line. Accordingly, by July, a concrete slab about fifteen by forty feet had been poured in front of the Section house. The combination of slab and shed roof altered the front of the historic building. In the May meeting of the Authorities, Scenic had requested these alterations to the Joint Executive Committee, only to have the idea rejected. Scenic obviously went ahead with the work. That, wrote Pyzel, was in violation of the lease agreement, Section (h), paragraph 24.

Pyzel also noted that Scenic began to convert one of the ex–Railway Post Office cars into a restroom for the Antonito yard. The Executive Committee, at the previous meeting, instructed Scenic to submit detailed plans before beginning the work. No plans were submitted and the work went on. In conversation with Robert Keller about these items, Keller opined that the conditions of the lease allowed Scenic "to make changes they felt necessary…he would make the decisions as the occasions arose and…he felt no compulsion to communicate with the Authorities." Pyzel believed that Scenic was disobeying the direct wishes and orders of the committee and that Scenic had withheld information and "demonstrated bad faith." He recommended that this whole matter be on the agenda for the July 17, 1973 Executive Committee meeting.

Well, running the diesel did stir up a lot of comment and criticism. The Authorities quickly pointed out that the contract, indeed the point of the whole enterprise, was to operate steam-powered excursions. Although Scenic had been allowed to use the diesel for a limited time in 1972, this did not permit it to use the diesel in subsequent years. Scenic disagreed, believing that the use of the diesel was "permanent." The New Mexico attorney general weighed in, writing that the use of the diesel was in violation of the contract. That, unfortunately, was only the beginning of more turmoil.

In July that year (1973), Robert Keller wrote a long letter to Chairman Ken Green of the Executive Committee. In it, Keller reported the results of Scenic's estimate of the economic "aspects" of proposed improvements to the railroad and just how those improvements could be addressed. Keller correctly noted that the future was still very uncertain, but he was willing to go forward on the basis of assumptions that showed "reasonable" profits when patronage reached 100,000 per year.

Keller concluded that only a few improvements could be justified at the moment. With ridership far below the very optimistic figure of 100,000, Keller wrote that only about $500,000 in improvements could be done by Scenic. The only way for more to be done was that rent paid to the Authorities be relieved, that the lease be extended and that a matching fund be established "to provide improvements." Therefore, Scenic would offer to spend the $500,000 on certain projects: a new Chama shop building (not to exceed $250,000), an Antonito track layout as shown in the master plan, the Antonito engine house, additional land in Antonito for camper parking (a new proposal, he wrote) and paving and landscaping at Cumbres. The work could be completed by the end of 1974 "if this offer is accepted before October 31, 1973."

The conditions set by Keller specified each state spending $250,000 on projects in Antonito and Chama. The work was to be done by the end of 1975.

Another condition was for the Authorities to grant four other requests: extend the lease for a total of fifty years and impose rent relief for twenty years starting December 31, 1973—the rent would be paid as per the present lease, except "that the two per cent portion shall have a maximum amount equal of 1000 adult fares and the minimum guarantee shall be eliminated." A third condition was to eliminate the bond requirement from the lease. Finally, there was an option to buy certain "excess" land in Chama for a proposed motel, at a price of $5,000 per acre. The option would end on December 31, 1976. There was one final caveat: all of the above depended on Scenic's upcoming stock offers amounting to sales of 200,000 shares.

The original lease of twenty years was set by state law in New Mexico, which prohibits leases longer than twenty years. The agreement with Scenic was specific, in that Scenic was to pay all property taxes, insurance and maintenance costs. Also, Scenic was to pay the states 2 percent of gross income, with a minimum payment of $4,000 the first year, $7,000 the second, $12,000 the third, $18,000 the fourth and $25,000 the fifth year (1976) and every year from then on.

Scenic's request for rent relief based on a 1972 adult ticket of $13.50 meant a payment of $1,350. At the time the lease was signed in 1972, Keller was quoted saying, "We think this is a very fair agreement," according to the May 14, 1972 *Albuquerque Journal*.

Fair or not, notes taken from the Joint Executive Committee meeting of August 21, 1973, just a year later, reveal the depth of feelings on both sides by now. Entitled "regarding maintenance of property," the exchange between members of the committee and President Keller grew very heated. There were accusations of lack of track work, bridge ties needing replacement, brakes not being tested on the trains and air pumps "all run out," with no work being done on buildings. Work was done on the lava pump house, Chama engine house, oil house and depot buildings, but no work was done on water tanks or bridges and the "cars were dirty and unattractive."

On July 2, 1941, the San Juan passenger train climbs toward Cumbres Pass near Coxo, Colorado, in the southeastern tip of Archuleta County, adjacent to the New Mexico line.

Keller responded by calling the lack of maintenance an "economic decision," that they were working toward a "viable business enterprise" that would lose about $70,000 in 1973. Keller must have felt the hot seat when accused of permitting the property to further deteriorate from last year. He responded heatedly, "This discussion is so much [BS], I can't believe it!!" He said that the operations were safe but that the overall condition was "deteriorating" and that was the "right strategy at the moment." When he was accused of "nearing the 'point of no return' by borrowing against future maintenance," Keller responded that such a point was a long way in the future. Track, locomotives, cars and structures were "major maintenance problems," and there were just no resources at the moment.

The acrimony continued, with further charges of unused ballast countered by Keller accusing the Authorities of not appreciating their effort to date, a charge denied by the committee. Keller hoped that the upcoming stock offer would be successful, and then much more could be done. Was Scenic in financial trouble, asked two members, and if so, could the states recover from deferred maintenance? Keller did not answer. Clarence Quinlan tried to mollify things a bit with comments about letting Scenic continue because the economies of both Chama and Antonito were already stimulated. That is balanced, he said, by the difficulty of getting money from both states. John Pritchard asked how Keller felt about operating trains with no maintenance. Keller responded that the advantage was to Scenic to operate because the committee was "overly concerned with maintenance, in three years Scenic will be on top."

A final comment from this meeting noted that Scenic would lose $100,000 in 1973, by Scenic's own projections. The $100,000 was a kind of bond "required under the lease" that reverted to the Authorities if Scenic elected to leave the property with no penalty. Its "departure could leave the Authorities with a rundown facility and no means to bring it up, even to the condition Scenic received it in."

Keller proceeded to defend himself in a letter to Authorities chairman Ken Green. He first complained of an unfair gross receipts tax on the money spent in the 1971 rehabilitation program. The amount was about $2,000. He pointed out that the original contract was a "cost plus 10 percent" deal. Scenic actually spent $20,000 more than agreed to, and by law, the gross receipts tax could be passed on to the customer. In this case, reasoned Keller, the consumer was the Authorities. Therefore, the Authorities should pay the tax. He also complained that approval of the food concessionaire at Osier was still not done.

Then Keller got down to the matter of the Executive Committee meeting and the derogatory comments alleged in the minutes of that August 21 meeting. He doubted that the quotes were indeed verbatim. But even if a tape recorder was present, those quotes were "taken out of context in a completely irresponsible fashion." He objected "violently" that the notes were even sent out. He said the record "must be set straight in this matter."

Keller further raised the continuing question of improvements to the property. He stated that should passenger numbers continue to rise, such numbers would soon outstrip the capacity of the railroad to carry them. He noted that alternative proposals called for would probably not be given serious consideration. That was a telling comment on worsening relations between Scenic and the Executive Committee. He went on to suggest alternatives to the present contract. He suggested that the states pay for all "necessary improvements; or, the states share with Scenic the expenses of improvements; or, finally, the states sell the railroad to Scenic 'on the condition that the improvements be made.'" He really preferred a sharing of costs but awaited action by the Executive Committee.

Much of Keller's justification of the information noted was based on the downturn of the 1973 season. Out of a total of 27,073 riders, only about 26,000 were paying riders. They had projected a season of 30,000. This meant a cutback of the number of trains planned for 1974, with a minimum of activity set for the winter of 1973–74. He said that 35,000 riders in 1974 was a break-even number.

In late December, Keller again referred to the economic situation. In a long, two-page letter addressed to the two state Authorities, Keller again asked for financial relief and/or support from the states. He wrote of fewer riders than projected, due to the gasoline shortage, and that any profit from operations in the near future "is now very remote." The same bleak view existed for any hopes of getting new capital, either from sales of securities or through borrowing, which were then much less than even six months earlier. He believed that the future was dim. The lease allowed Scenic to quit the lease if losses were in excess of $100,000 for any five-year period. Its losses, he wrote, were much more than that in only two years. Keller wrote that operating losses for three years, 1971–73, were $19,687, $35,446 and $138,058, respectively. He also noted that Scenic improvements were $26,946 for 1972 and $36,167 for 1973. The total of losses and investments amounted to $256,304. This figure, when combined with other investments, including the buses and other equipment, came to total expenditures by Scenic Railways of $397,200. He believed this figure to be larger than that of either state's investment.

The investments by Scenic might be returned in 1974 if passenger levels were close to forty thousand. Given the unstable circumstances of the gasoline shortage, however, Keller wrote that they were expecting a season of only five thousand. Fear of the unknown led Scenic "to prepare for the worst." He again hoped for an easing of the financial burden of the lease with financial aid from the state, as well as unstated changes in the lease to Scenic's benefit so that, among other things, the sale of common stock might succeed.

On December 31, Keller again wrote to Ken Green. Keller's intention was to ask that the rent check due to the Authorities not be "negotiated until such time that the C&TS RR reaches a self-supporting patronage level." He referred to the forty-thousand-passenger level and its losses as creating a "severe shortage of operating capital." Banks that had loaned money in the past would not do so then. If the check were cashed, he wrote, it would take action by the legislatures to pay the money back to Scenic. Therefore, he hoped that the whole matter could be taken up in the January 1974 meeting of the Authorities. In light of the uncertainties then, Keller said that he would withhold the check until after the meetings. Only then would he deliver the check. He was obviously assuming a favorable vote on rent relief for Scenic.

Scenic management and employees did demonstrate yeoman service that summer when emergencies arose. In July 1973, for instance, the air compressor on #483 quit, and the run from Antonito was cancelled. Something had to be done, and something was done. In Antonito, tours were arranged for waiting passengers. In Chama, #484 was quickly fired up and, in two hours, was on the way to Antonito. One fireman had to ride the bus from Antonito to Chama to serve as engineer, with Scenic employee Gary Getman firing. The Antonito passengers were given the

Taken in July 1947 by Bert H. Ward, this image depicts a westbound San Juan passenger train stopped near a water tank and amid servicing. Note the World War II–era jeep to the left.

choice of waiting for #484, with an estimated 6:00 p.m. departure, or riding the following day. While pondering this offer, Scenic's shop crew drove from Chama to Antonito, replaced the air compressor with another from a display locomotive (it is still missing, a common practice in the past), completed the work and tested it. To a cheering crowd, the compressor functioned. Locomotive #484 arrived an hour later. The train, now with two locomotives, left at 6:00 p.m. for a double-head out of Antonito, an oddity in itself that late in the day. The two locomotives were separated at Osier. All the riders were fed there, and the run continued through the night. The entire consist arrived in Chama at 12:30 a.m. About one hundred tired and cold passengers appeared "spirited and happy."*

Cooperative efforts of the volunteers with Scenic's staff continued work on various projects on the railroad. Restoration and lettering of the mileposts and restoration of some of the telegraph shacks, with new roofs and painting, were among those projects. The car attendant program continued to provide service to the passengers.

With it all, the successes, troubles and rising level of acrimony between Scenic and the Authorities only revealed how bad things were getting. Something happened, however, with the volunteers' attitudes contributing to the coming of big troubles. There were no newsletters from September 1973 until January 1974. More problems were to come, some of which were beyond the control of any of the agencies involved in the C&TSRR. As noted before, the war in the Middle East stopped oil delivery to the West, creating massive economic dislocation. Particularly hard hit was the American tourist industry and, therefore, the Cumbres & Toltec Scenic. The oil embargo lasted from October 1973 to March 1974.

Notwithstanding these economic troubles, the C&TS did operate. On January 12, Scenic did put on a display of snow fighting. Rotary OM, built by Cooke Locomotive Works in 1889, ran as a winter special. While a great experience for rail fans, it was not a financial success for Scenic. Its employees donated time and effort to prepare both the rotary and the necessary locomotive to power the train. Also, both state legislatures prepared to appropriate $100,000 each for maintenance of the railroad. Finally, that spring, Scenic made a public stock offer of $5 per share, with a minimum sale of one hundred shares. This would not prove to be a successful way to increase its capital supply. Troubles were only beginning.

CHAPTER 5

MORE TROUBLES

S cenic announced plans for the 1974 season with fewer trains than in 1973, use of the diesel and no steam until later in the season. The "Pineapple," Oahu Railway #19, was scheduled to run from Cumbres Pass to Sublette and return. This short, nonsteam train would run one round trip four days per week, departing at 10:30 a.m. and returning by 4:30 p.m. on Saturday, Sunday, Tuesday and Thursday. Fares were eleven dollars for an adult and four dollars for children under twelve years. Steam operations would return on August 3 and run through October 6 from Chama on Saturdays and from Antonito on Sundays. A total of only twenty steam trains were planned. All of these nonsteam and reduced steam trains was due to the "gasoline crunch." This kind of abbreviated program was noted with a "hue and cry" in the press, among rail fans and in state agencies. The New Mexico attorney general joined in pointing out that the lease called for steam only and that the use of diesel was only temporary. Steam must be used. Scenic countered, asserting that the lease allowed permanent use of the diesel. These arguments continued to poison the atmosphere.

All was not completely lost. Another movie (*Bite the Bullet*) was shot on the railroad, providing some income above that generated by passenger revenues. The movie meant a lot of cosmetic painting and carpentry. Locomotive #483 was given an earlier look with black and gold trim and red paint on the drivers. The Hinman coach received similar treatment, giving the coach the appearance of a business car from the 1870s, and was lettered "The Western Press Special." A horse barn structure was also built in the yard just north of the historic engine house.

Also in Antonito, Robert Burggraaf was arranging for land and funding to build a two-stall engine house in the coming year—part of the present four-stall building. This work was in accordance with Scenic Railways' Master Plan and was to be completed by July 1974. The previous turning wye was to be replaced with a balloon loop, as well as appropriate track and switches to serve the new engine house. In short, despite economic dislocations and an abbreviated schedule, the picture appeared optimistic for the coming year.

The volunteer organization continued to grow, with new chapters being formed (Los Alamos and Chama, New Mexico, and Denver, Colorado). The Denver chapter was made up of many from the Colorado Railroad Museum at Golden, especially the noted founder of the museum, Robert W. Richardson. Headquarters, however, were still located in Albuquerque. The volunteers continued to offer the car attendant program in support of the railroad and made other material contributions: paint, lights for the Chama engine house, more car attendants, paint for the bunkhouse and so forth. All in all, the volunteers were making a good impression on the property. The NGRRA board of directors met once a month. The treasury had a balance of $2,250. There was some criticism in the newsletter, warnings that printing unsubstantiated rumors or innuendo would only lead to trouble—these were prophetic warnings.

Trouble again developed, however, over the use of diesel instead of steam power. Members of the Railroad Authorities continued to point out that the contract with Scenic called for steam power exclusively. This was despite the temporary use of the diesel in 1972. The New Mexico attorney general also determined that Scenic was in violation of its contract, but no action was anticipated for the moment.

The Bicentennial Committee also continued with plans for the railroad and Chama. In order to acquire matching federal and state dollars, the committee needed to raise some of its own money. In pursuit of the funds, a July 6 moonlight excursion was organized—specifying the use of steam power. The committee planned an evening passenger run from Chama to Cumbres Pass behind two locomotives that would be accompanied by a barbecue dinner at the pass. There were plans for photographers to disembark in order to photograph the train. All would be well fed and happy for the return, a moonlight descent from the pass to Chama by about midnight. The best-laid plans…

The Bicentennial Committee also had ambitious plans for a new depot at Chama, reinstallation of a turntable and other appropriate developments in the Chama yard. The historic depot was to become a museum. Plans went ahead for the moonlight train ride. This was to attract more fans and serve as a fundraiser for the Bicentennial Committee projects.

Starting in late December, Authority consultant Dan Pyzel began writing a notebook of "Weekly Reports." He did so until January 31, 1975. He reported that Robert Burggraaf was acquiring land and funding for a two-stall engine house in Antonito. The funds would also provide for a turning loop to replace the cumbersome turning wye. In 1974, the movie *Bite the Bullet* was filmed, with several alterations and temporary movie sets remaining in the Chama yards. Scenic promised to remove the changes, but that did not happen for several months. One change occurred with the painting of the historic caboose for the movie. The volunteers of the NGRRA agreed to repaint it. Unfortunately, wrote Pyzel, they used a very "unsuitable" color of red, which did not come close to a more appropriate "freight car red," a color used by the D&RGW in the past. The volunteers offered that this particular color was available and might also attract more riders to the train. A caterer for the lunch at Osier was selected, Port of Call. Its staff prepared to use the historic section house as a kitchen, with *al fresco* dining on picnic tables. All was still not entirely well, however, since water had to be hauled from Antonito every day.

Scenic started off the year with the Supreme—a steam-powered snowplow special from Chama—to rail fans' delight. Rotary OY was the last of the rotary plows used by the D&RGW, and that was in 1962. So, this promised to be a really spectacular operation. In 1972, the volunteers did exterior work on the rotary. In the winter of 1973–74, off-duty C&TS employees brought the machine up to operating condition. Fifty ticket holders rode the train, with opportunities to take pictures at regular stops. Many more crowded the highway for the same opportunity. A good time was reportedly had by all. Things looked better for the new year.

As noted previously, the Chama Bicentennial Committee stepped in with a plan, approved by Scenic, to run a special, steam-powered moonlight run for July 6. Departure from Chama was scheduled for

6:30 p.m., with photo run-bys, an arrival at Cumbres by 8:00 p.m. and a barbecue feast there. Daylight Savings at that time of the year, in the high mountains, usually meant plenty of daylight for the feast. The return trip would be by moonlight, with arrival back in Chama at midnight. All did not go well, however. The number of tickets exceeded the space available. Therefore, two cars were brought down from Cumbres, which caused a delay.

Management reportedly claimed that late coal deliveries caused the delay. It also claimed that 7:30 p.m. was the actual departure time. Be that as it may, the train departed then and immediately ran into difficulties. Weeds and unused track, with rust, straw and a spray of grass seed and mulch used by a contractor to stabilize loose earth caused by highway construction, caused the wheels of the locomotive to slip and stall. Attempts to utilize the sanders on the locomotive were futile. Reportedly, the sand was left in the locomotives over the winter and, hence, would not flow down onto the track. The crew eventually resorted to hand-sanding the worst spots. All of this was combined with "injector trouble"—the devices by which water is injected into the locomotive for conversion to steam. Cumbres was reached by 10:30 p.m. By the light of bonfires, hungry riders devoured the overcooked barbecue of elk—at least those riders who could stomach the strong flavor of overdone elk. The train had finally returned to Chama by 2:30 a.m. Bicentennial chairman Jim Demlow reported that one-third of about three hundred who rode had a good time.*

This same summer, another agency from New Mexico appeared to become a major player in the future of the C&TSRR. In 1966, the U.S. Congress passed the National Historic Preservation Act. With this move, each state was mandated to prepare and enact suitable laws in compliance. In New Mexico, the action of the governor and legislature produced the Cultural Properties Act, which, in turn, created the Cultural Properties Review Committee (CPRC). The committee was, and is, composed of historians, archaeologists and architects, two each respectively. The legislature also created the positions of state archaeologist and state historian, each associated with appropriate state agencies—the Laboratory of Anthropology and the newly created State Records Center and Archives. By 1972, this committee and its support staff were up and running, nominating historic structures and districts to the State Register of Historic Places and more deserving sites to the National Register. In 1974, the committee became involved with the railroad. In 1972, the C&TSRR was placed on the National Register of Historic Places.

At the regular monthly meeting, in June 1974, Dan Pyzel and John Pritchard, consultant and member of the New Mexico Railroad Authority, respectively, appeared before the CPRC. Their presentation consisted of a general explanation of circumstances and a slide presentation. The result was the creation of a subcommittee, dubbed the Railroad Committee, to represent the interests of historic presentation as a part of this grand but troubled undertaking. From then on, one or another member of the CPRC attended Authority meetings, reporting back to the CPRC for action. The relationship of the CPRC to the New Mexico Railroad Authority was defined by the attorney general as having the authority to "inspect all…Cultural Properties…[to ensure] integrity and proper maintenance" and the power to order compliance. The AG went on to write that both state laws "apply to the operations of the C&TSRR."* Within a short time, the CPRC approved a subcommittee report, "Historic Preservation Guidelines," for the railroad, laying the groundwork for the future.* In September, the CPRC asked Vernon J. Glover to prepare a historic preservation plan in recognition of his background as a railroad historian.

By the end of operations in 1974, Scenic Railways had asked the New Mexico Railroad Authority to provide financial relief from those payments required under the lease. Under the lease, Scenic Railways was supposed to pay the states $12,000 as part of the "rent," plus $7,500 for taxes and insurance. Another $4,500 was required by a separate provision of the lease due the Authority from the 2 percent of Scenic's gross receipts. Authority member John Pritchard said that only $4,500 of the "rent" would be required, in exchange for a promise that Scenic would run thirty trains in 1975. Scenic said that the request was due to financial troubles brought on by declining riders because of the energy crisis. And the issue of using the diesel continued to dog Scenic. Furthermore, nothing could be done until the Colorado Railroad Authority agreed to the plan. Finally, an appropriation by both legislatures for money to improve the railroad could not be spent until slightly different language between the two bills was ironed out. It seems that neither bill specified that monies from each state's appropriation could be spent in the other state. That would have to wait until legislative sessions in 1975. This was another clear indication that the present arrangement with the two separate Authorities was cumbersome and quite unworkable.

There were also some voices raised in criticism of the NGRRA Board. The Denver chapter letter in the December issue of the *Telltale* pointed out the lack of communication between the board and the Denver chapter members. Of particular importance was the preservation of the historic character of the railroad. Fears were raised that the property might turn into a copy of Disneyland or Knott's Berry Farm. The writer pointed out the historical resources available in the Denver area: the Colorado Historical Society, the Colorado Railroad Museum and the very headquarters of the D&RGW. One particular point of concern addressed the fear that the NGRRA was strictly a New Mexico organization. The Denver people felt left out. The editor's response was a promise to look into the various matters. There would be more trouble in the future.

As noted earlier, the concern over the use of diesel and questions raised about maintenance of the locomotives, rolling stock and structures persisted throughout the latter half of 1974. Both chambers of commerce, Dan Pyzel, interested fans, Antonito town trustees, area newspapers and advisory letters from New Mexico's attorney general all combined in a rising chorus of criticism of Scenic Railway Inc. Questions of terminating the lease were addressed as early as May of that year on the basis of maintenance and safety. Robert Keller, president of Scenic, responded in defense of using the diesel by arguing that diesels were used before the state's purchase:

> *We also feel that Railroad Authorities are empowered by the lease, under section three, to allow any use of the premises which—in their opinion—is consistent with the basic use of operating steam powered passenger excursion trains. Since subjective judgement is required to interpret the word "consistent" (a synonym of "harmonious") in this usage, we believe that the Railroad Authorities are the only bodies which may properly rule on this point. We believe that the question cannot be considered on legal grounds alone…We believe that the advisory letter states a subjective opinion and not a legal opinion, and therefore should*

*be withdrawn. The letter has damaged both our ticket sales and common
stock sales efforts.*

Keller asked that the advisory letter be "withdrawn." That request was
refused. This acrimony carried over into the next year in a big way.

As the new operating year of 1975 dawned, nobody was aware that
everything was about to go downhill. Both Scenic Railways and the
NGRRA were about to experience problems—external ones for Scenic
and internal ones for the NGRRA. Even the New Mexico Railroad
Authority had its share of internal squabbles.

A special insert in the spring 1975 edition of the *Telltale* screamed,
"Train May NOT Run This Year!" What followed was a lengthy account
of the February meeting of the New Mexico Railroad Authority.
The Authorities had earlier in 1974 contracted with the Ken R.
White Company, a private engineering company out of Denver, for a
comprehensive inspection of the entire track, bridges, culverts, switches,
ties, bridge timbers and tunnels. That report called for extensive track
"repairs" in order to ensure safe operations in the coming year and
recommended that no trains be run until such "repairs" were completed.
Scenic claimed that it had "repaired" the track to better condition than
when received. Steve Reynolds, New Mexico's state engineer, felt that the
"repair" work was required under Scenic's contract.

The word "repair" was featured in the contract. The interpretation
of "repair" was the crux of the situation. Scenic claimed that it had
"repaired" the track. The states, on the other hand, noted that the White
report clearly showed the need for more repairs. So, the states had to be
satisfied as to work done before safe operations could continue. Therefore,
no trains could run. Scenic wanted the two states to appropriate enough
money to bring the line up to Class 2 standards—the Federal Railroad
Administration standards for all mainline railroads. Those standards
allow passenger train speeds of up to thirty miles per hour and freight
train speeds of up to twenty-five miles per hour.

Reynolds, an experienced and highly respected water engineer in his
own right, pointed out that even if the states could agree on spending
state funds to fix the railroad, it was a violation of the contract—another
attorney general's opinion would have to be handed down. Then, even if

permission came from the New Mexico attorney general and the money was approved, Colorado would have to approve, too. This meant a joint meeting of the entire Authorities, something that was difficult to do in so short a time. Short of that move, there would have to be a lease amendment, and that would take time.

Scenic thought that the Authorities should go ahead and approve the money, even if this was illegal. That idea was quickly laid to rest, since the Authority members were probably personally responsible for any illegal expenditure. The White report did point out several thousand defective ties along the mainline, on sidings, at switches and so forth. There were missing bolts, fishplates and the like everywhere. Tunnel No. 1, the so called Mud Tunnel, was subject to land movement that affected timber supports. All of this was in contrast to Keller's stand that Scenic would not spend one more cent on "capital" improvements.

The same flyer reported some confusion in the New Mexico Railroad Authority, due to the resignations of Dan Pyzel, Terrence Ross and John Pritchard. All three referred to "personal" reasons, lack of state support and general feelings of deteriorating relations with Scenic management. There were also differences of opinion between the Colorado and New

Locomotives #487 and #495 pull an eastbound D&RGW stock train from Durango, Colorado, in the Chama depot area. These locomotives were K-36- and K-37-class engines. The photograph was taken in the early 1950s by Robert W. Richardson.

Mexico members. At a previous meeting, the members of the Joint Executive Committee agreed that there would be no more requests to either attorneys general without prior agreement by the committee. But the New Mexicans did, in fact, go back to their attorney general for another opinion. This created a hiatus in a subsequent meeting. In fairness to Ross, Pritchard and Pyzel, relations with Scenic were difficult, likely due in part to Scenic's rather poor public relations. A negative attitude was not the best way to handle members of interested historical parties. Joe Vigil, of Chama, was appointed the new vice-chairman of the New Mexico Railroad Authority.

In other actions at the same meeting, the CPRC historical guidelines were presented and approved over the objections of Scenic Railways. After that action, the members listened to a proposal by Vernon J. Glover for a historical research project. This would lead to a survey of the property, rolling stock, tools, buildings and so forth and result in a basic historic preservation plan. His idea was adopted, with sources of funding to be investigated. With this unhappy exception, the mood was generally depressed.

Subsequently, Scenic employee and NGRRA member Gary Getman, in an open letter to the NGRRA members, took strong issue with the information in the flyer. Calling the flyer "muckraking journalism," "half truths" and "the most colored piece of journalism"* in his letter, Getman refuted point by point the assertions of the flyer. He asserted that Keller's statement about capital improvements was policy that predated the track report. The track report was made to determine condition, not safety. The report recommended that $50,000 be spent early in the season and a second similar amount only "if the states want to bring the track up to a FRA class 1 status." There was no mention in the report that this would have to be done "before a wheel turned." He correctly pointed out that State Engineer Reynolds was a "water resource" expert and knew nothing of railroads. (Reynolds had emphasized his credentials at the time the CPRC was drawing up its guidelines.)* Getman especially questioned why any responsible person would urge an illegal transaction in an open meeting. There were a few final criticisms aimed at the editor, urging him to report facts and leave his own opinions out. All of this showed how relations between Scenic, the Authorities and the members of the NGRRA were declining.

Later that spring, in 1975, NGRRA president Jim Case wrote an open letter to the members. He pointed out the obvious problems in the relationships and purposes of the two organizations. The NGRRA members, some of whom were instrumental in the saving of the railroad, were dedicated to the preservation and restoration of the railroad. Scenic, on the other hand, was a for-profit company, dedicated to operating the railroad as a piece of narrow-gauge history. Case then referred to unnamed differences over the recent years that had caused "ill feelings" between the two groups. The railroad, he pointed out, is owned by the two states and was "public property." Scenic Railways Inc., however, was under contract as the legal operator of the property and therefore could legally control public access. That meant that volunteers were allowed on the property *only* with Scenic's permission. Therefore, he hoped, a good working relationship could be restored to the benefit of both interested parties.

Scenic Railways was the legal operator of the C&TSRR, under contract to the Authorities and was subject to the contract. This meant the NGRRA had *no* legal agreement with either the Authorities or Scenic Railways Inc., and therefore the NGRRA was in no position to make demands on either of those parties. Since the early days of operations, Case reminded the members, the volunteers had provided the car attendants. For the most part, this had worked to the benefit of all. The car attendants were not in a position to voice opinions about the operations of the railroad or to criticize Scenic Railways operations; they were there to help the riding public and provide any aid requested by Scenic employees. If and when there were questions of operations or safety, the proper avenue of recourse was through the monthly meetings of the Authority. Case closed by reporting that, in recent talks, Scenic Railways' management had indicated a continuing welcome to the volunteers.

In this same issue of the *Telltale*, John Oldberg, superintendent of Scenic Railways, laid down the new rules for the car attendant program. While he praised the attendant program and hoped for more in the future, Oldberg effectively created a new group, totally separate from the NGRRA and subject to his supervision. Clearly, Oldberg was in charge of the car attendant program, run now by Scenic. An editor's note in the *Telltale* emphasized that this was a new group of volunteers, formed by

A westbound passenger train leaves Osier station on October 21, 1950, photographed by Robert W. Richardson. Osier is situated on the headwaters of the Rio de los Pinos, which cuts the gigantic Toltec Gorge a few miles downstream, or east.

Scenic, and had nothing to do with the NGRRA. The NGRRA activities now were limited to historic preservation and publication.

All was not quiet in other matters. This same newsletter reported that the Denver chapter was stirring with new interests "after a long winter of internal problems." Denver members were working on projects in Antonito. The *Telltale* editor also answered a letter asserting that the insert in the previous issue ("Trains May NOT Run This Year!") had an "unfortunate choice of title." Lastly, a letter signed by Scenic employees expressed support for the operator. The letter, they wrote, was of their own doing and was not sponsored by management.

Topping off a bad time for NGRRA was a letter to its members from Robert Richardson, of the Colorado Railroad Historical Foundation in Golden, noting various discrepancies and complaints directed at him, the Colorado Museum and Colorado, in particular. He noted that he was delighted to see the line saved and that the museum was open to any and all for historical information or any other help. When charged with not helping to get the line open, he noted a complete lack of communication from the NGRRA. He went on to point out needed work, such as painting and so forth. Significantly, Mr. Richardson noted that he had paid dues twice but was not shown on any list of members. (This would not be the last of such queries.) He hoped that the money went for some useful purpose. He was a member of the NGRRA for many years. This meant that he was in association with model railroaders and a second group he labeled "model railroad politicians." He wrote that "the latter [were] a sizeable and too often fractious minority. I strive to avoid the latter." He urged the NGRRA to support the C&TS into prosperity. Too many rumors, he said, were damaging and should be stopped. The NGRRA would struggle on for three more years.

In 1975, the volunteers did initiate an ambitious project to restore enough rolling stock to form a prototypical "Freight Train." A total of sixteen representative cars were selected to make up one or two typical freight trains for display. The group started with a special fund for materials. Volunteer money was to be matched with CPRC funds and, hopefully, a federal match in 1976. Refrigerator car #166 was given the first treatment, with scraping, a "Cat" yellow painted on the sides and "Tuscan" red on the ends and roof. "Reefer" #163 was next in line for similar treatment. There were also further delays in sending membership cards due to personal problems of the NGRRA membership director and lack of a substitute, but things seemed to continue with some success.

By that fall and winter, the two "Reefers" were completed ahead of schedule, and stock cars #5691 and #5706 were also completed, although there was a labor shortage that delayed some work. Rumors continued to float around that the NGRRA had ceased to exist, but continued publication of *Telltale* stopped those stories for the time being. Criticism of Scenic Railways also continued to surface in the same paper. Merely by quoting certain passages from the lease, it implied Scenic's noncompliance with certain provisions. For instance, reference to the lack of preservation of historic buildings, maintenance of other structures and the like suggested noncompliance. By the end of September, Scenic Railways had carried just over twenty thousand riders, far short of an anticipated break-even point, now estimated to be fifty thousand. Finally, near the end of the season, the NGRRA Board decided to publish six issues of the *Telltale* in the coming year: February, April, June, August, October and December. This was a rather ambitious schedule for any volunteer group.

The last issue of the *Telltale* for 1975 carried a color photograph of the two newly painted "Reefers." The final number of riders was 24,770, noted John Oldberg. Plans were again laid for Scenic employees to volunteer to prepare Rotary OM for one run in February 15, 1976, and the 1976 season was planned to start June 12 and run through October 10. Still, in all, the final issue for the year contained letters of mild complaint about the lack of communications between volunteers and Scenic employees, talk of not running in 1976 and the editor's denial of such, saying that the train merely *might* not run. He ended with a call for a "clean slate" in 1976 and to "*forgive and forget.* Both sides have a *lot of growing up* to do!"

Sadly, the newsletter did not appear in the following year until July 1976. That was the last issue of the *Telltale*. Although some key NGRRA personnel were lost due to job transfers, the car attendants continued to function, although the car restoration project faltered. A plea for help showed that time was running out for the NGRRA.

Through the next three years, 1976–78, there were increasing numbers of letters directed to the Albuquerque address of the NGRRA from new members complaining about the lack of newsletters and lack of renewals being acknowledged. Further indication of breakdown of administration of the club was the number of membership and donation checks sent in that were neither cashed nor returned. By 1978, mail was being forwarded from the usual address to another without any action being taken except to put the checks and the mail in a file. Membership cards were returned (one torn in half).

Finally, a special meeting of present and past members of the NGRRA was called for December 11, 1978, in Albuquerque. The sole purpose of the meeting was to dissolve the Association and to disperse "all assets and property." The notice also informed the membership that the assets, including some funds, were to be transferred to the Historical Society of New Mexico, a nonprofit agency, such assets to be used for "railroad preservation and restoration."* For the next several years, the historical society handled publications through its newsletter, *La Cronica de Nuevo Mexico,** and the board of directors created the Railroad Committee to handle publications and preservation projects on the C&TSRR.

CHAPTER 6

A DECADE OF CHANGE

1978–1988

C hange was in store not only for the volunteer movement—it would be gone by 1978—but also for the Authorities and the operator. Experience had proven beyond a doubt the clumsiness of the administration originally established by the states. The awkwardness of two Authorities, joined together by the joint Executive Committee, had demonstrated the need for something better. In 1974, Congress approved the Cumbres & Toltec Scenic Railroad Compact, which the states had created that year. The problem lay in the lack of ratification of the compact by the two states after Congressional action had created it.

Through 1976, both state agencies labored to create an interstate agency. Finally, on July 1, 1977, the legislatures of both states created the present Cumbres & Toltec Scenic Railroad Commission, an interstate agency as originally authorized by the compact. This new commission was now composed of four members, two from each state, appointed to serve at the will of each governor, with an executive director. There was no more "consultant," nor large unwieldy bodies separated by differing and, on occasion, conflicting state laws. The results were immediate and impressive. A single body now supervised and controlled the railroad.

Another looming change, unrecognized at first, resulted from financial difficulties for the operator. Constant calls for rent relief by Scenic revealed the kind of financial crunch it was experiencing. Continued criticism of Scenic for using the diesel as motive power for the trains further soured the atmosphere, and the numbers of riders had never come close to dreamed-

Engine #493 pulls a long freight train near Cumbres station, which includes flat cars carrying lumber and pipe.

of projections earlier that same decade—twenty-five thousand per season was far short of Scenic's projected break-even figure of fifty thousand. As a result, the Authorities, and later the commission, had relieved Scenic from paying the annual rent; a fee based on the number of riders was cut to a symbolic one dollar per year. This move meant that the income formerly derived from the operator's rental payment to the Authorities/commission was not now available for upgrading the railroad. The only other sources of money available to them were from the state legislatures or grants from suitable organizations, federal and private.

Scenic Railways continued to struggle on. In 1977 and again in 1978, the Railroad Authorities agreed to reduce Scenic's rent to $1 per year. In 1977, Scenic Railways reported a net operating profit of $77,051. That same year, President Gerald Ford signed the bi-state compact. Scenic also reported on a new board of directors on February 1, 1978. Mr. Boyd West of Los Alamos, New Mexico, became general manager. He replaced Robert E. Keller, who had resigned as general manager. Keller had quit the position as the result of "internal problems"* but remained on the board of directors. Other members were John Oldberg, superintendent; Clovis Butterworth, passenger agent; and Cissy Martinez, office manager.

A Decade of Change

The Operating Department was headed by Oldberg, with Bernie Watts as shop foreman, Rich Broden as senior engineer and Max Pacheco as track foreman.

The previous year, 1977, Scenic reported on expenses incurred with the six International Harvester buses purchased in May 1973. The original purchase price was $132,000.00, or $22,000.00 each. This debt was financed at $2,801.01 per month for a period of sixty months and $110.00 per month for an additional twenty-four months. The final payment was calculated to be $13,182.60. This was a very heavy debt load. In 1977, Keller estimated the value of the busses to be $8,000.00 each. Executive Director Carlton Colquitt reported to the Authority in Santa Fe on February 28, 1977, that Scenic grossed about $500,000.00 in 1976. On October 19, 1977, Keller wrote to the Colorado auditor, perhaps anticipating criticism, to the effect that "if the lease is not well understood, the audit report may well be seriously flawed."* Later that year, 1977, the Colorado attorney general waived the 2 percent payment for 1976, but not for the succeeding two years of 1977 and 1978—despite the recent decision of New Mexico to reduce the rent by a different figure.

On February 28, 1978, Keller and Scenic president William Earl Bell wrote a long, six-page letter to the Colorado state auditor thanking him for "providing us with the pre-release copy of your report on [Scenic's] operation of…the railroad." In this lengthy report, Keller and Bell noted that the auditor's report suggested "that the C&TS RR might be operated on a financial basis more favorable to the States." Scenic responded with the conclusion that in order to achieve this goal, it would have to raise fares. About half the riders, it noted, were from the two states. Any fare increase would "weaken the already-tenuous marketing position of" the railroad.

With this thought in mind, Bell and Keller embarked on a review of the states' involvement and the "benefits which have accrued" since Scenic took over operations in 1971. They noted that officials in each state and some in the press had opposed the original purchase by the states. Much of the criticism at the time was directed at the improbability of the operation ever being a financial success. The fear was offset by the fact that the original purchase price was essentially the same as the scrap value of track and equipment. In the ensuing years, the price of scrap metal had risen until the states could see a greater value than when purchased. In short, the cost of failure could be offset by sale for scrap.

Furthermore, in 1970 the property and equipment were in very run-down condition. This was evident in photographs taken at the time.

All of this led Bell and Keller to make the comparison between the run-down condition in 1970 and the many improvements evident by 1978. "Substantial improvements" had been made since work began in 1971, the first year as a tourist attraction. That year, two locomotives were prepared (conforming to Federal Railroad Administration rules), ten freight cars were converted to passenger cars and "considerable" work was accomplished on track and other facilities. The physical plant in 1978 was much improved, thanks to repairs made by Scenic and the states, and was now "unquestionably 'a going business.'" Scenic's invested capital was very much at risk in proving or disproving the "validity of the enterprise." Its capital had been spent in start-up expenses (losses), improvements to the property and part of equipment acquisition. The 1973 Arab oil crisis almost caused all of this investment to disappear. By 1978, the states and Scenic Railways, having demonstrated the railroad as a viable business, had attracted the infusions of federal, state and

An eastbound freight train crosses Cascade Bridge on August 8, 1951, not far from Osier, Colorado.

operator-financed improvements, all of which meant that the railroad could be now sold at a "substantial profit."

Meanwhile, back in 1973, a new engine shop had been built in Antonito, with financing provided by several interested individuals and with "ancillary support" by Scenic. Many of the same folks prevailed on Gene Autry, the "singing cowboy" of Hollywood, to donate D&RGW locomotive #463 to the town of Antonito.*

Scenic had expanded passenger service after 1972 by putting into service nine more passenger cars while rebuilding and upgrading the ten previously modified cars. Two locomotives had been overhauled since 1976, along with other substantial repairs carried out, all at Scenic's expense.

The total payroll from 1971 through 1976 further indicates the economic impact of the railroad on the region. This amounted to about $720,000. Various government agencies approved a little over $1,600,000 from 1971 up to June 30, 1978. During the same period, through 1976, Scenic spent more than $1,700,000 on "improvements, maintenance, promotion, insurance and operation of the railroad." And for the same period, Scenic suffered losses of about 10 percent of "revenues."

In those government monies was $596,000, granted by the Economic Development Administration for construction of a new passenger depot at Antonito, track and roadbed work, as well as the new shop building in Chama in 1973. All these improvements contributed toward making the railroad a much better tourist attraction. The economic benefits to Chama and Antonito, and the states at large, were evident.

Scenic's claimed losses of $172,751 were all in the auditor's report. All indications, said Keller and Bell, pointed to steady growth and benefit—assuming no other economic crisis or natural disaster. All of this would continue in a favorable manner as long as the fare structure could be kept under control. In short, they wanted no fare increases. The fares charged on the C&TS were, at the time, on the order of 50 percent higher than the Silverton Branch of the D&RGW (now the Durango & Silverton). Higher rent to the states, coupled with increased levels of capital improvements, required higher fares. Higher fares would be undesirable—"counter-productive from a marketing standpoint." They, Keller and Bell, "strongly disagreed with the auditors' suggestion that 'more favorable' economic benefits to the States be negotiated."

Scenic Railways continued to plead for a reduction, or at least only a nominal payment, in the annual rent charged by the commission (states). This was the ultimate death knell for Scenic, if it continued to run trains only on a limited basis. In 1978, it ran another winter snowplow (souvenir badges are in the Friends' collections).

In September 1980, Scenic's president, David B. Ogle, wrote a long essay entitled "The Cumbres & Toltec Scenic Railroad: Lessons of the Past, Plans for the Future." In thirty-one pages and seven appendices, Ogle tried to set the company's house in order through a look at the history of the project. He discussed the basis for the state's purchase of the railroad, reviewed the first ten years (1971–80), noted that the 1980 operating season was a "Test for Future Planning" and ended the discussion with "Lessons and Conclusions." Having built his case with a ten-year review, Ogle went on to talk about development of future goals with specific proposals. Finally, he disclosed a closely held company secret that told of internal discord within the company's board of directors and the final resolution of that discord, as well as other matters.

Scenic's experiences in operating the railroad through those first ten years of state ownership compose the story of the C&TSRR up to the end of 1980. At that point, Ogle pointed to five conclusions:

(1) *"Without major changes to the physical plant and a reorientation of state and company objectives, significant growth in patronage cannot and will not occur. Future planning must be based on the concept of zero growth."*

(2) *"The economic survival of the railroad is dependent upon keeping operating expenses proportionate to revenues."*

(3) *"No amount of advertising or sales promotion effort will solve our growth problems."*

(4) *"Private ownership of the railroad would almost certainly result in its rapid failure, due to excessive maintenance, debt service and interest expenses."*

(5) *"Future public or private funding, if either is forthcoming, must be judiciously targeted toward a maximum return in the problem area we have identified."* The above mentioned trouble within the company and the above five points.

Having said all that, Ogle opined that there were only two alternatives: the states should run the railroad through direct subsidies, or there must be new thinking about turning the railroad from a "one-day amusement site into a terminal recreational complex" that would attract visitors for several days or weeks at a time. This concept of a "terminal" attraction occupied the final pages of his paper.

Thereupon, Ogle elaborated on the twin themes of "Historic Preservation" and, in his words, "Economic Stimulation." Up to this date, he noted, preservation of the historic buildings, rolling stock and the whole atmosphere of a historic railroad had received short-term stabilization and preservation. Interestingly, he recommended that preservation "can be most properly handled via…a state-sponsored, non-profit historical foundation." The lack of any significant operating revenues always left matters of historic preservation without funding. Ogle went so far as to identify this author as "the Commission's very capable and sensible Historian," receiving Scenic's "strong endorsement" to "spearhead this future effort."

Ogle then went on to explore ideas for a destination site. "Scenic Railways believes that many unique features of the Cumbres & Toltec—its remote and beautiful location, its built-in capability to carry people to a scenic site without their automobiles, and its historic 'theme'—offer an exciting opportunity for development of a destination resort." The suggested name for the resort was Railcrest Ranch.

The most important condition, said Ogle, was to negotiate a new and much longer lease. This was not the first time Scenic had broached the subject. Now, in light of a proposed ranch, a lease of thirty-five years was necessary in order to amortize "real property improvements over a 30-year span." Construction might not start for five years, hence the need for a longer lease. The new lease was an absolute "must" before Scenic could commit to this plan.

It should be pointed out that there were other projects associated with the development of the ranch. The public facilities at Antonito offered a significant opportunity for improvement—with additional lodging and dining facilities. There were also other sites considered overlooking Toltec Canyon and Phantom Curve, "but track construction to the site is difficult." That site was the rimrock above Toltec Gorge. Cumbres Pass was also considered, but the too-easy highway access was thought to be a disadvantage. Scenic hoped to carry all visitors by train to the ranch.

As finally decided by Scenic Railway's planners, the proposed ranch would be located on "Osier Knoll"—located "on a rounded hill overlooking the mainline about one-half mile east of Osier." The site permitted "construction of a level reversing loop...with track access feasible from both directions." Upon arriving by train, the guests would find three classes of accommodations: a commodious lodge of 15,000 square feet with sixteen motel rooms, ten "dual living units" and "twenty converted narrow-gauge boxcars equipped with RV fixtures and large outside decks!" Guests were to be treated to the usual array of "dude ranching": fishing, horseback riding, hiking and backpacking, jeep tours, nature walks, staff theatricals and so forth. Interestingly enough, the resort proposed to remain open throughout the winter. The fact that Osier is located at 9,600 feet above sea level in open country with constant winds seems not to have entered into their planning.

Railcrest Ranch would not be the first of such developments; as Ogle noted, other railroads had pioneered resorts along their lines—Sun Valley, Idaho, for example, by the Union Pacific Railroad.

The last matter in this rather amazing document, as noted earlier, concerned a crisis within the company's board of directors. In early 1980, its board engaged in infighting that was never "fully revealed to the Commission." The major question concerned which "operating format would produce the most desirable results for the company's shareholders." There were two sides to the issue. On one side were those who favored the two-train format, the one ultimately adopted, as the best way to operate the railroad at a profit "and seeking other long-term solutions to developing a broader revenue base." The other side wanted to operate fewer trains, using the round trip from Cumbres Pass to "drastically reduce operating costs and 'bring the Commission to its senses.'" The "Cumbres Turn" had operated during the 1973–74 oil crises and was very controversial. There was also "talk of liquidating the company in order to preserve some of its investors' capital."

Things were, according to Ogle, at an impasse that "could not be suitably resolved by parliamentary means...Heated discussions took place, replete with accusations of executive malfeasance and threats of lawsuits." The existence of the company was in jeopardy.

A committee composed of Bell, Ogle and Watson met independently of the other members to resolve the matter. This group, favoring the two-train/"non-confrontation philosophy" came up with a plan. The "company faction" bought the stock of the other faction, composed of Keller, Baur and Dahlin, all of whom held the proxy of Ms. Shirley Lindholm, and these three agreed to resign from the board of directors and to execute "unconditional releases" from any claims against the company or the remaining directors. The size of the board was reduced to five, which streamlined the board and made decision-making easier. Two new members were elected, a new president was also selected and the company's financial control was "vested in a compatible Board."

"Scenic Railways," wrote Ogle in his September 1980 essay, "has now put its house in order. We stand ready to undertake the substantial future tasks outlined in this report." The Cumbres & Toltec Scenic Railroad "can still become one of the world's most unique and successful recreational attractions."

But in 1981, Scenic's days in the San Juan Mountains were almost over. At the end of that season, Scenic came forward with another request for rent relief. That was "the last straw" for the commission, and it cancelled the contract with Scenic Railways in late 1981. The stated reason was declining revenues for three consecutive years. The original contract noted that a period of three continuous years of declining revenues permitted the cancellation of the contract. Executive Director Colquitt was already in consultation with another operator, Kyle Railways Inc. of California.

Kyle Railways owned and operated some dozen short-line railroads and several tourist lines, all in the western United States. One notable tourist line is located on the island of Maui in Hawaii: the Lahaina, Kaanapali & Pacific Railroad, also popularly called "Sugar Cane Train." Willis Kyle, the founder, had been in the steel industry long before becoming interested in railroads. Kyle & Company was a steel distributor and fabricator with plants in Fresno and Stockton, California. The company was involved in extensive shipbuilding during World War II. In 1951, Kyle & Company was bought by Pittsburgh Des Moines Steel. In 1956, Willis Kyle bought Federal Steel and Supply in Fresno. At the same time, he happened to be in a San Francisco bank that, he noted, was auctioning off an eight-mile railroad. This was part of an estate sale. As more of a lark than a real business venture, he offered a "conservative" bid that was initially rejected, only to be accepted a week later. (His was the only bid.) Mr. Kyle, to his great surprise, was now the owner of the Yreka Western Railroad in Siskiyou County, California. Later, in 1986, the national Christmas tree was taken from a forest of the Sierras in California. It began its journey to the White House on the Yreka Western Railroad. This was the beginning of Kyle Railways.

Since that first purchase, Kyle had bought branch line castoffs from one or another mainline railroads or, in the case of the bankrupt Chicago, Rock Island & Pacific, major parts of the line in Kansas and eastern Colorado. A former lumber railroad operating out of Cottage Grove, Oregon, served for a few years as a tourist carrier when the timber business of the Northwest began to decline. The other tourist ventures were the California Western out of Fort Bragg, California, and the previously noted LK&P line in Maui. He quickly became known among his colleagues as "Mr. Short Lines, USA."

Mr. Kyle's professional activities included serving as Pacific regional vice-president of the American Short Line Railroad Association and chairman of the board's Executive Committee, and he was on the board of directors at the time of his death. He was honored as "Man of the Year" by *Modern Railroads* magazine in 1987. Kyle Railways brought all of this activity to the C&TS in 1982. It was an experienced company with the kinds of resources needed to make the C&TS a bigger success than it had been under Scenic's direction.

Also in the early 1980s, another change came to the C&TSRR. A new volunteer movement emerged from the shadows of the old NGRRA and the still active Railroad Club of New Mexico. Albuquerque attorney William J. Lock and his friend Glenden Casteel persuaded then general manager Joe Vigil of Chama to allow the two access to the Chama yard to repair and paint the historic caboose #0503, among other pieces of rolling stock. Lock's buying and reading the recently published *Historic Preservation Study* sparked this activity. Lock's eager involvement led to Joe Vigil discussing with this author, over lunch in Chama, the possibility of reviving the volunteer program. In September 1981, Lock invited Clif Palmer, then public relations agent for Scenic Railways, to give a presentation of a short film about the C&TSRR to the Kiwanis Club of Albuquerque. Lock also wrote to me in Socorro to ask to share the speaker's table for Palmer's presentation. All was well received, and from that event came luncheon meetings with Wilson and Lock in Albuquerque, virtually every Friday, up to the present.

The San Juan passenger train pulled by locomotive #478 crosses the Lobato Trestle in New Mexico near the Colorado line.

Lock's powers of persuasion led to establishing annual work sessions in Chama, along with the subsequent luncheons. Lock was former president of the Kiwanis Club of Albuquerque. Drawing on that experience and the concept of "sweat equity," Lock incorporated that idea into the new volunteer effort. At the time, I served on the board of directors of the Historical Society of New Mexico, a private nonprofit organization, and was very active in promoting the study of the history of New Mexico and the Southwest. Subsequently at those luncheons, Lock and I discussed finding a suitable organization to serve as an umbrella agency so that we could recruit volunteers, raise money and buy materials. The first step was to get Lock elected to the board of the historical society in the spring of 1982. President Albert E. Schroeder formed the Railroad Committee as a permanent committee of the board. The new volunteer group was in business—in a manner of speaking. We had few members, no money and a lot to do. Fortunately, in early 1983, an anonymous donor gave the Railroad Committee a grant of $1,000 to get started.

For the next several years, the volunteers operated under the auspices of the historical society, soliciting money and members and organizing the first work session in Chama. There were not enough workers to go anywhere else along the railroad, so the restoration of Cumbres, Osier and Sublette and facilities at Antonito would have to wait. But their time was coming. In the early years, the numbers grew slowly. Nevertheless, the committee announced the formation of an ad hoc group, known then and now as the Friends of the C&TSRR. The historical society acted as the parent organization, handling its funds and publicizing its activities in the society newsletter, *La Cronica de Nuevo Mexico*. Work sessions in Chama continued for the next several years until the newer Friends was formally organized. The early years of this new group would serve to convince both Kyle management and the Railroad Commission to give wholehearted approval to it and the later Friends group, but that had to wait.

By May 1988, there were sixty-one members in the Friends group. Lock and I knew that the time had come for us to spin off a new organization with better name recognition, which would mean an increase in memberships, more money, more workers and more work of historic preservation. At 10:00 a.m. on March 12, 1988, the "organizational meeting of the Board of Directors of the Friends of the Cumbres & Toltec Scenic Railroad, Inc." convened in Lock's office in Albuquerque, New Mexico. We were in business. Over the next several weeks, we incorporated, by-laws were written and adopted, publicity was organized and a logo—the current one—was designed. That May, an operating budget was adopted, membership brochures were designed and ordered, preparations for upcoming work sessions were made and, most importantly, the name for a newsletter (the *Dispatch*) was chosen. The 1988 budget showed total income at $2,540 and total expenses at $2,486, a balance of income over expenses of $54.

At the 1989 work session, more than one hundred people appeared, coming from various parts of the country and working on many projects from Chama to Alamosa plus on invaluable and unique rolling stock, such as Derrick OP and its tender flat car. In 1991, the Denver & Rio Grande Western Railroad donated two 1910 standard-gauge boxcars for a display of both narrow- and standard-gauge equipment in Antonito.

This was just the beginning of acquiring historic rolling stock as a part of the Friends restoration projects.

Returning to 1982, the earliest work sessions had been organized under the auspices of the Historical Society of New Mexico. Over the next several years, the numbers attending those work sessions grew from the original two, Bill Lock and Glenden Casteel, working over one long weekend to two weeklong sessions of more than three dozen people. By August 1987, there were forty-four folks from all over the country—California, New Mexico, Colorado and even Florida. Both the Railroad Commission and the operator, Kyle Railways, endorsed two work sessions. Lock worked with General Manager Dan Ranger and Kyle corporate attorneys to hammer out a legal agreement. The volunteers agreed to insurance coverage for their members while working on the railroad in order to avoid potential claims against the operator or the commission.

Those first work sessions were devoted mainly to painting and repairing rolling stock. There were bigger projects in the offing, but they had to wait for more personnel and more detailed planning. In short, there was still a lot to be done. On the other hand, the visual effect was noted early on. Mr. Kyle, on one of his periodic visits to the property, mentioned to Dan Ranger that the property was looking so much better. Dan said that it was all due to the work of the volunteers.

As noted previously, by 1988 the time had come to form a new, independent organization with name recognition. The Historical Society of New Mexico had served to help and encourage the work of the volunteers, but membership had remained rather static, with perhaps only two dozen railroad volunteers within the much larger general membership of the society. Therefore, in March 1988, the incorporating meeting was held in Bill Lock's office. The by-laws were adopted, the newsletter was started and an annual meeting was scheduled for August 10, 1988, in Chama. At that meeting, the first board of directors was to be elected. The by-laws called for sixteen directors to be chosen from among those interested in the railroad to represent the "constituencies that make up the members of the Friends." Of the sixteen directors, eight were to be elected for two-year terms, and the other eight for one-year terms. From then on, eight directors would be elected for two-year terms. Finally, the by-laws provided that the officers of the corporation be elected by the board of directors.

The Cumbres & Toltec Scenic Railroad's K-27-class engine #463 and K-37-class engine #497 are shown parked at Cumbres station.

Seven of the initial directors were from New Mexico: Glenden Casteel of Albuquerque, who was one of those responsible for the resurrection of the volunteer program in 1981; Russell Fischer of Chama, who was operations manager for Kyle Railways; William Lock of Albuquerque, another of the original founders of the volunteers; Claude Morelli of Albuquerque, a teenage volunteer in 1983; Dan Ranger of Chama, general manager for Kyle; Laurie B. Schuller of Placitas, a civil engineer and longtime volunteer; and your author, Spencer Wilson, professor of history, who recently served as one of the New Mexico Railroad commissioners.

Seven of the Colorado directors were Carl Carlson of Denver; John Carson of Grand Junction, retired carman for the D&RGW (more than forty years), active volunteer and invaluable teacher for the new volunteers; Chip Irwin of Denver, active volunteer and designer of the current logo for the Friends; Darlene Phillips of Aurora, an active volunteer; Leo Schmitz of Antonito, executive director of the commission; Charles Slovacek of Antonito, active volunteer; and Hugh Wilson of Denver, active volunteer. Two additional members came from both coasts: Dr.

Fred Knight of Cherry Valley, California, a dentist by profession and volunteer since 1983, and Calvert Smith of Jacksonville, Florida, also an active volunteer. All of these folks were destined to contribute in their own significant way to the volunteer program and to the railroad.

On July 10, 1988, the board met in Chama to plan for the future, including the annual meeting and elections. The potential board members drew lots to determine who was to run for one-year terms and who for the two-year slots. There was one other change before the elections: Hugh Wilson dropped out due to business reasons, and Joe Vigil of Chama filled his position. Vigil was a former general manger for Scenic in the last days of its operations and came with other impressive credentials from various business interests.

At the same time, 1987–88, there was another major development for the C&TS. The 1987 season saw a total of 38,721 people ride the train, the best year so far. For all of the riders, the high mountain scenery, spectacular vistas and the experience of riding a steam railroad through these high mountains was exciting enough. There was one bit of a "let down." The dining facilities at Osier, the regular lunch stop, bordered on the primitive to nonexistent. The only structures were the section house, a small depot—converted to bathrooms—the water tank, stock pens and the remains of a coal loading dock. Scenic had recognized early on that something was needed.

One of the first actions by Scenic was to convert the section house into a kitchen facility, with an additional extension of the roof to cover the food line for buffet-style service. The customers were then expected to (and did) seat themselves at picnic tables, with spectacular views of the Rio de Los Pinos canyon. Spectacular views, however, did not compensate for continuous wind or worse. I can testify to horizontal sleet and wind that, on occasion, blew the food off the paper plate. I could hang on to the tray and plate but not all three.

Something had to be done to shelter the passengers, but what? There were no other buildings there suitable for handling two hundred or more people for a lunch hour. Various ideas were floated about, by the means of many extended phone calls, from rebuilding the covered turntable to portable buildings and even tents. All such suggestions required considerable manpower to erect such structures in the spring and dismantle them in the fall. A rebuilt covered turntable, with open sides, only invited the wind tunnel effect, and if the turntable were enclosed, then teams of workers would be shoveling accumulations of snow from inside the next spring. All these problems were finally resolved with a permanent, covered and heated dining facility. Design work started. There had to be a plan before the commission could approach public and private agencies for funds.

The commission hired Akira Kawanabe, a well-known and respected architect from Alamosa, to design and supervise the project. His original plans called for a two-story building, with serving area, dining area and restrooms on the main floor. The lower floor would contain the kitchen, souvenir shop, storage space and additional dining area. The main entrance was to face the railroad tracks to the east, while the west side overlooked Rio de Los Pinos and the canyon toward Cumbres Pass. The total cost was estimated at slightly more than $500,000. Funding came through the states, $170,000 each and $45,000 from private foundations (the Boettcher Foundation, El Pomar and Mountain Bell). The commission, through the cooperation of Kyle Railways, raised the

This fireman's-side view of the Cumbres & Toltec Scenic Railroad's locomotive #497 with freight is located at the siding leading to Tanglefoot Curve, just east of Cumbres station.

balance by the implementation of a $2 surcharge on adult tickets sold during the 1987–88 seasons. This amounted to $127,800. Mr. Kyle's initial objections to the continuation of that surcharge faded rapidly when he became aware of the improvement in the passenger's experience that resulted. He never raised the matter again.

The bid process began in mid-May 1988, with the expectation of awarding a contract by early June. Things did not go that smoothly, however. Bids came in way too high for the funds available. Due to the remote location, all material and labor costs were considerably higher. As an example, concrete delivered in Antonito cost $60 per yard, but at Osier the charge was $100 per yard. The large, 250-foot glued-laminated trusses came from the U.S. Northwest by truck, and Leo Schmitz, executive director of the commission and successor to Carlton Colquit, described the trucks' descent from Osier Peak, down the winding forest service road, as "interesting."

So, at subsequent meetings with Kawanabe, the scope of the building was scaled back with less expensive finishing touches, such as the elimination of a balcony on the river side and so forth. The basic size and appearance remained the same. Finally, on July 6, 1988, the commission approved a contract with Commercial Building Services Inc. of Denver for a total of $528,653. Work began on July 11. Footers were poured, but because of delays, construction was halted for the winter and was resumed as soon as possible the following year. A completion date was set for August 15, 1989. Finished in time, there was room for four hundred people to eat inside at tables without food blowing off and rain diluting the meal. A sharp rise in the number of riders over the next few years was attributed almost entirely to the construction of this facility.

There was one downside to events in 1988. In June, a movie company accidentally burned Cross Bridge, which lies about five miles west of Antonito. Also known as "Hangman's Trestle" or "Ferguson's Trestle," the bridge's name stems from the lynching of a man named Ferguson by the folks of Antonito sometime about the turn of the century. There is no explanation of Ferguson's misdeeds, but lynch him they did; apparently, the trestle was the highest place for enough elevation for the rope and the bad guy.* The film starred country western star Willie Nelson, who was also making a TV western called *Where the Hell's That Gold?* On June 13, special effects were designed to represent the destruction by fire of the bridge, but things got out of hand and it burned to the ground. A contemporary photograph shows the special effects man holding his head as he realized that one fire extinguisher was useless for an eighty-foot trestle completely engulfed in flames. The railroad was forced to shut down for six days, for which it was compensated. The film production company built an emergency culvert so operations, and also the movie company, could resume their respective works, and at the end of the season, the present wooden reproduction was installed at the movie company's expense.

By the end of 1988, despite the burned bridge, things had really changed for the better on the railroad. The new facility at Osier was under construction. The Friends group was demonstrating willingness and capacity to make significant changes to the property, and the number of riders was increasing. As ridership increased, so did the memberships in the Friends.

CHAPTER 7

A DECADE OF CHANGE, FOR THE BETTER

1988–1998

As noted, there were several important changes in the late 1970s and the early part of the 1980s. The streamlining of the administration of the railroad through the introduction of the new commission as the governing body, replacing the inefficient Railroad Authorities, was a major step forward. Secondly, the new body of dedicated railroad volunteers, including some members of the previous group, and the continuing efforts of the Railroad Club of New Mexico brought new vigor, expertise and administrative skills to the project. Finally, a new operator was introduced that also brought increased railroad experience and substantial financial and industrial background. It was a time of increasing optimism and growth. In short order, as the number of riders began to increase, Kyle Railways increased maintenance on both rolling stock and track and roadbed work. The volunteers, first under the auspices of the Historical Society of New Mexico and the Railroad Club of New Mexico, later emerged as a new organization, the Friends of the C&TSRR, Inc.

In early 1988, the Friends numbered over 110 members. By the end of that year, there were 174 members, and the Friends Board continued with a program of volunteer work sessions on the railroad, sponsored special trains as fundraisers and published books on railroads (some new publications and others as reprints) as a means to raising money. As required by by-laws, the annual membership meetings were held in Chama as part of the work sessions. Kyle Railways began rewarding the work session volunteers with a free ride as far as Cumbres Pass. All these elements were met with great enthusiasm. The 1988 work session brought 74 people to volunteer their time labor at their own expenses on the railroad.

Details of the 1988 work session accomplished in Chama yard included painting and repairing buildings; repairing running boards on refrigerator cars, idler flat cars and pipe gondolas; window repairs on the Chama engine house; and so forth. The scale house and access pit were cleaned, painted and repaired, and new wood was added to the scale house and pit. Maintenance of way work was summarized by Director Cal Smith for the August work period of twelve days as a donation of 360 man hours. The work included preparing, priming and painting fifty-nine mileposts and whistle boards, and fourteen whistle boards and ten mileposts were installed at their proper locations. Ten more mileposts and five whistle posts were numbered in place.

Kyle track crews, led by Max Pacheco, transported volunteers to positions along the right-of-way. One part of the maintenance of way crew departed early from Antonito, working along the line by truck under the direction of Executive Director Leo Schmitz. Crews, arriving in four-wheel-drive vehicles, used ladders dropped off by the train crew and painted the support columns for the lava water tank. Other line-side

This side view of C&TSRR locomotives #463 and #497 shows them pulling freight cars near Lobato.

crews worked from Cumbres to Osier and from Chama to the Cresco highway crossing. At the end of the work session, the crews enjoyed the train rides provided by Kyle. The point of all of this detail is to show the careful, although sometimes chaotic, planning and cooperation between the volunteers and Kyle's crews. Quite literally, neither could have accomplished the work without the other. This was only the first instance of close cooperation between the Friends and Kyle, a symbiotic relationship that matured during the years of Kyle's operations, and this was only the first year of the new volunteer organization! Better things were to come.

Operations continued with an ever-increasing number of people riding the train. Hollywood continued an active interest in using the railroad for various movies—both full-screen and made-for-television. (Then and now, Hollywood has made motion pictures on the railroad. It's a valuable source of public exposure and nice extra income. See a list of those movies in *Ticket to Toltec.*) Kyle also restored four of the former D&RGW locomotives to service. In 1989, the Friends organized the first "Moonlight Special" for members and the public as a fundraising special. Those trains, then and now, departed Chama in midafternoon, stopped for a "run-by" for photographers and arrived at the new facility at Osier for a steak dinner cookout. The return trip started after sunset so that the trip could run by full moonlight, arriving back in Chama at about eleven o'clock. Friends members act as car attendants to answer questions and to lower and raise stairs in the boxcar coaches. The occasion of a running train, long after dark, brought out many folks from their summer cabins—there had not been a night train for many years. That first "Moonlight" train ran to rave reviews. An unexpected event on one of the early "Moonlights" added to the aroma when the train hit a skunk.

In 1988, the Friends newsletter, the *C&TS Dispatch*, was first published, starting in Bill Lock's office. Later in 1988 and 1989, the *Dispatch* came under the direction of Editor Art Nichols, with expanded offerings, the new logo, membership information, a list of directors and a schedule of events. A new feature in 1989 was the occasional addition of articles on railroad modeling.

In 1989, work again resumed on the dining facility at Osier. Winter snows make work and access impossible at 9,600 feet above sea level. As soon as the road into the site was cleared of snow and dried out in late spring, work resumed. The project was completed early in the 1989 season. The new dining hall was dedicated on Friday, June 30, 1989. Among the two hundred people at the dedication was United States representative, and current governor, Bill Richardson of New Mexico. (From that meeting came the moves by Carl Turner of Santa Fe to ask Richardson for federal dollars to restore locomotive #463—the "Gene Autry" locomotive. Autry had donated the engine to the town of Antonito, but funds were not available locally for its restoration. At the dining hall dedication ceremony at Osier, the Antonito Town Council sold the locomotive to the C&TS Commission for one dollar. In time, thanks to Congressman Richardson and New Mexico senator Pete Domenici, the federal money came, and #463 runs today.)

Other activities that year included Steven Spielberg filming another movie on the Pueblo & Chama Railroad: *Indiana Jones and the Last Crusade*, released later that same year. A Friends work crew in August 1989 went to the abandoned rail yards at the Public Service Company of Colorado power plant in Alamosa. The project was to dismantle and remove the last three-rail switch in Alamosa (indeed, the last anywhere in the Rocky Mountains) for eventual display in Antonito. Three-rail track permitted trains of standard gauge (four feet, eight and a half inches) and narrow gauge (three feet) to operate on the same track sometimes with cars of different gauges. Dubbing themselves the "F Troop," the Friends work crew dismantled the switch, albeit with great difficulty due to lack of expertise, proper tools and greatly corroded metal. A few years later, with help from Kyle track crews, the crew installed that same switch in the Antonito yards for all to see. Unfortunately, it cannot be used due to extreme wear of the switch "points" (the "points" guide the wheels from one rail to another through the switch).

A second major project that year, among many, was restoration work on the snowshed at Cumbres Pass. When the states bought the railroad, a very impressive structure (a wooden "tunnel") existed over the turning wye at Cumbres Pass. The purpose was to keep the deep snows of winter from covering all of the tracks at the site. This arrangement of switches and sidings permitted operations to continue during the winter, allowing the turning of helper locomotives and snowplows as the principle purpose. At one time, there were extensive sheds covering much of the track at Cumbres, but by 1979, only one remained. It was 400 feet long and covered one switch, the tail of the wye and a coaling station. The wooden structure was probably never treated with wood preservatives and received minimal maintenance. In 1979, almost three-quarters of the shed "fell" down. This left a 103-foot, 6-inch section still standing. Starting in 1989, plans were made to stabilize and repair that remaining portion. Measurements were taken, structural engineers consulted and a plan drawn for the next summer work session. It was the prototypical example of the type of careful planning the Friends group did before any work was done.*

Furthermore, projects were designed to be carried over from one year to the next. For instance, Derrick OP and the accompanying boom tender car #06063 called for the carpentry and car repair crews to be combined for the 1989 August work sessions. On the derrick, crews removed rigging and appliances, as well as the old wood from the deck. Historically accurate decking materials were installed and finished with oil treatment. The old roof of the engine house on the derrick was replaced with proper siding, canvas and sealant. Other details were also replaced, including a new set of doors for the derrick "house." The boom tender car also had new decking installed. Even some of the old bolts were saved and reused when one volunteer (Roger Breeding) rethreaded the old bolts and retapped the old nuts, allowing their reuse.

New oak sills replaced the old, thanks to various suppliers, including a company in Kentucky. The skills of retired D&RGW employees such as John Carson and Harry Babcock were essential for this kind of detailed woodwork. Those two taught other volunteers how to handle difficult freight car repair jobs such as installing a "scab" or a "dutchman" and replacing of the end sill with all mortises and holes, including the four truss rods. A significant amount of additional work on the derrick and boom tender car was carried over to the 1990 season. Details, such as recoating the roof of the derrick "house," painting inside and out and reinstalling doors and some minor parts of the brake rigging were done. More work was planned for the next season. Finally, spray painting the old cars was fast and relatively easy compared to what had to follow: the re-lettering of those cars. Special crews (then and now) painted and re-lettered. These first years, the volunteers were playing "catch-up" with paint especially. Decades of neglect required hasty action on their part to stop and hopefully stem the effects of use and weather. The combination of harsh winters and equally harsh summer suns is devastating to wooden surfaces. The volunteers had their work cut out for them in paint alone—painting is never ending.*

By December 1989, membership in the Friends group had risen to more than three hundred, as noted by President Bill Lock in the December issue of the *Dispatch*. Membership growth allowed the volunteers to even more "promote and preserve the Railroad."

In summing up the 1989 work session, President Lock referred to all of the projects and characterized the work done as "plugging the dike," as well as stated that the Friends group was moving on to historic preservation and restoration. The second "Moonlight" train was, he noted, a fundraising effort and becoming a tradition—as it still is. Another such special was already scheduled for July 1990. The 1990 season was the beginning of the second decade of the new volunteer effort; much was accomplished but more was coming. President Lock referred to the probability that missing historic equipment might be returned to the property. It was an optimistic appraisal for the coming years.

Indeed, that same year, the Cumbres line and the Friends attracted a visit by Mark Smith, editor and publisher of *Locomotive & Railway Preservation* magazine. Mark became a leading voice in the railroad preservation movement for as long as the magazine was published. Beginning in March 1986 and continuing to the last issue in March 1997, he documented "the preservation and operation of historic railroad equipment." He first visited the railroad in 1985 and again in 1990. (The second issue of the magazine—vol. 1, no. 2, May–June 1986—featured the C&TS and the volunteers.)

The '90s visit was at the invitation of the Friends. Mark arrived on Thursday, August 16 and spent the next few days (until the following Monday) touring the entire length of the railroad. Friday was spent driving to the most remote locations: Osier, Sublette and the Los Pinos pump house, as well as Antonito. Sitting on the hillside at Sublette while train #1, the Colorado Limited, pulled in with a track crew and speeder waiting on the siding, was a very moving "railroad experience." From Sublette, he took the very unimproved road down into the Los Pinos Canyon and to the pump house, where water was pumped at one time up to the lava tank. Mark was extremely impressed with this very solid basalt structure. He discussed with your author and Leo Schmitz the future of such historic structures on the C&TS.

Since Mark had never been to the Antonito yards, he was particularly anxious to visit. At the time, locomotive #463, the "Gene Autry," was stored in the engine house. Outside, a group of volunteers, "F Troop," was re-laying the three-rail display track—removed in previous years from the old power company yards in Alamosa. He tried his hand at driving spikes…and actually hit them. The return to Chama meant a stop at Cumbres Pass to watch the volunteers working on the section house, the car inspector's house and the snowshed. His visit continued on Saturday, getting acquainted with volunteers, talking shop with Kyle crews, taking lots of photographs and generally observing the volunteers at work.

Sunday was most interesting, with a general but informal discussion. Mark thought that this discussion meeting was of special significance in light of the relatively short lifespan of the Friends. He commented on the activity generated, the ideas tossed around and his impression of a very active and focused volunteer group. He also got to ride the newly restored Derrick OP in a short maintenance of way train, departing Chama west to the end of line. Engineer Gerald Blea put on a special run with plenty

Locomotive #497 of the C&TSRR pulls freight cars west of Lobato Trestle in New Mexico, near the Colorado line, illustrating why "Scenic" is part of the railway's title.

of smoke and whistling. In his remarks given on Saturday evening to the volunteers, he commented on the Friends having "tremendous enthusiasm and energy…Our house is in order." With "evident integrity in…projects," the Friends "have avoided a narrow focus…We [You] are attempting a comprehensive approach to preserving and interpreting the C&TS." His parting remark summed up his impression: "Today it's not just the equipment we're saving—it's a way of life. We who preserve aren't just antiquarians…we're saving things that serve the spirit, things that will create a richer future."

In that same issue of the *Dispatch* was a letter from Carlton Colquitt, once consultant to the Joint Executive Committee of the old Railroad Authorities and later executive director of the commission. In that letter, Colquitt also noted the emergence of the "new" volunteer movement after the demise of the first group. Credit, he noted, always went to that first group, which saved the railroad between 1968 and 1970. This new volunteer group "appear to be serving an equally important task of providing popular support which not only expands the preservation effort, but also [ensures] that elected officials continue to support the railroad." Little did Mr. Colquitt, or any of the others, realize the truth of that statement by the end of that decade.

Finally, in that same issue of the *Dispatch*, there appeared a letter from George Swain, member of the Railroad Club of New Mexico, member of both "old" and new volunteer groups and a railroad historian in his own right. In that letter, Swain noted the success of the present movement:

I feel our success is a result of four special things: 1. We have a historically significant and interesting collection of equipment and tradition in a spectacular mountain setting; 2. We have outstanding leadership. Volunteers are cherished and made to feel cherished…work sessions have allowed team building to take place; 3. We have a good relationship with the Commission and Kyle Railways, and with the communities of Chama and Antonito; 4. We have been able to take advantage of good luck and to minimize the effect of bad luck. The safety program is effective, teams care for one another and discourage the person who does rash things…an outgrowth of the high esteem in which each volunteer is held, we attract and keep outstanding craftspersons. I very much cherish the leaders and craftpersons that we…enjoy.

Truly, the Friends group was developing into a first-class operation with first-class people.

The same kind of first-class organization was true of Kyle Railways. Since taking over operations in 1982, Kyle had worked to improve operations and maintenance of rolling stock and track work and increase the numbers of riders. One of the first actions by Kyle was to sell the busses that Scenic had purchased and used. (Kyle turned to leasing twelve passengers vans for the operating season, thus avoiding the debt load occasioned by owning the busses year round.) Kyle also began operating trains on a daily basis from Chama and Antonito. General Manager Dan Ranger pointed out one day that "every thing was in place, why not run every day?" So they did. That meant, of course, that the buses were unneeded and the attendant debt burden unnecessary. The busses went to a school district in southern New Mexico, and the trains ran.

Kyle also began a more aggressive program of locomotive maintenance during the winter months. Kyle could call on experienced employees and other resources associated with its other operations. Increased locomotive work ultimately resulted in six locomotives being in operating condition, plus the former U.S. Navy diesel #19, nicknamed the "Pineapple." Equally true of Kyle's locomotive activity was the emphasis placed on track, tunnel, bridge and roadbed maintenance. Some of this work was paid out of various grants, both private and public, but Kyle also contributed, as with the two-dollar surcharge added to the ticket price later in its tenure. All of this created an atmosphere of change for the better. The number of riders grew, at a slower pace than wished for, but the numbers increased nonetheless.

One of the most awesome activities on a steam-powered railroad, be it narrow or standard gauge, is the running of the rotary snowplow. Winters can be very harsh in the San Juan Mountains along the border of Colorado and New Mexico. Snow accumulations at Cumbres can exceed eight to ten feet on the level, with twenty-foot snowdrifts! In the active days of the D&RGW, trains running twice a day would tend to keep the road open. Of course, there were those times when the snow stopped operations for days at a time, even weeks in one instance, covering the train or causing wrecks. Rotary snowplows were invented in the 1880s because of such heavy snows in the high mountains of the American West. So it was on those occasions, both when Scenic was operator and later with Kyle, that a snowplow train was called out to clear the line in time for summer operations. (There are those times when conditions of sun and warmer weather lower or practically remove the snow before the season opens.) When the snow accumulates during the winter, with no trains running, the twin actions of thaw and freeze turn the snow into ice, making removal even more difficult.

In 1991, the combination of a heavy winter and a late spring snow required the snowplow to open the line. On a weekend in May, alternating between bright sun and blizzard conditions, Rotary OY and a supporting work train attacked heavy drifts below Windy Point. Finally breaking through the last ten- to twelve-foot snowdrifts, the train made the yards at Cumbres Pass. There the crew plowed out the main siding and one leg of the wye (because of the direction of travel, only one leg of the wye could be plowed—a chilling reminder of the necessity of having a snowshed-covered wye). The train tied up at Cumbres for the night.

The next day, bright and sunny with blue skies, a second train departed Chama. This was the Rotary Snowplow Passenger Extra, with two hundred ticket payers on board. This extra train was sponsored by the Friends organization, partly for publicity and also to raise money. It was an example of the growing partnership between Kyle and the Friends. Willis Kyle was in attendance. He did fret somewhat about the expense! The extra train stalled just below Windy Point due to icy rails—it still got very cold at night in the high country. Rescue came from the snowplow train, backing down, around Windy Point, coupling on the Extra—with both locomotives pulling, they reached the summit. The schedule called for the Extra to return to Chama. It did not leave the Los Pinos Valley, however, until the rotary train was observed working through snowdrifts on the opposite side of the valley. A lot of happy fans and photographers returned to Chama. (There were those fans who regretted eating tainted food the night before.) The work train went on to Rock Tunnel to clear the last major drift. During the following week, a second work train proceeded on to Big Horn, plowing out a few small drifts and clearing debris before returning to Chama. The road was open. The event was again a display of the close working relationship of Kyle, the Friends and the commission that was a mark of that decade.

The summer of 1991 saw another element of Friends activities on the railroad. Summer work sessions were organized for June and

August, with a total of 80 folks in June and a record of 109 in August. The July *Dispatch* noted the extent of work during that first session and included a reprint of a short article by noted railroad historian John H. White Jr., of the Smithsonian, concerning "Restoration." The Friends group was already following the guidelines promulgated by the National Park Service and under the watchful eyes of the historic preservation programs of both states. But the matter of just how much restoration would take effect was always a debatable subject. So, for the sake of interested readers, here is that short message as first printed in the July–August 1988 *Locomotive & Railway Preservation*:

> *Radical Left: Believers in radical surgery favor this method of cutting away all of the old tissue when removing a cancer. Any part of the old fabric that shows the slightest wear is removed and replaced. Small blemishes, cracks, and holes are enough to condemn a piece. Everything must be made solid and like new.*
>
> *In the Middle: Those who abhor extremes favor removing only the most battered or rotted pieces. When possible the more solid part of badly worn pieces will be saved by a skillful splicing with new material. Holes, cracks, and dents are repaired and made to blend in with the old surface. The major goal here is to made the object look neat and well cared for but not necessarily like new.*
>
> *Radical Right: According to the less-is-better school, nothing much beyond prayer should be undertaken when treating historic objects. The arrest of corrosion and decay is a high priority. Even cleaning is done at a conservative level. Mechanical repairs are made only if necessary to stabilize and hence insure long-term preservation. After the work is completed, the object, looking no better than it did before the process began, is put in a safe environment free from pollution and sunlight.*

Opinions may vary, but the Friends attempt to follow the middle road.

Another element in the Friends developing programs concerned adding to the collection of historic equipment and rolling stock. In previous years, the Friends recovered, moved and installed a three-way switch in Antonito, along with a short section of three-way display track close by. In 1991, the first in a series of additions to the collection came to the property. Since 1984, Bill Lock had worked on acquiring two historic standard-gauge freight cars, which were still standing on isolated rail in the Alamosa yards. These two cars were built in 1916 as standard steel boxcars. In time, after long service, they were relegated to maintenance of way tool/material cars and finally ended in Alamosa as lowly storage cars. These cars were moved to Antonito, restored to their appearance as revenue boxcars and placed on the three-rail display track along with the standard-gauge idler car. The final step in this process was the result of an agreement between Friends, Kyle and the commission and saw the restored cars donated to the commission—as was the practice in the future (a matter pertaining to insurance coverage of the whole collection since private cars are not allowed on the property).

The summer of 1991 saw even more restoration and preservation activity by the Friends. In Antonito, the aforementioned standard-gauge boxcars and the idler car were installed, painted and lettered. The idler car had all the rotten decking replaced with new decking and the mechanical aspects repaired and made operable, with final mechanical repairs, painting and lettering set for the 1992 season. The isolated mountain section town of Sublette received extensive repairs, with new roofing on the section house, for instance. Both state historic preservation offices allowed the use of asphalt shingles, for much longer life compared to wooden shingles. At Cumbres Pass, the section house was also repaired and painted. The very dilapidated car inspector's house was in dire need, with most of the roof gone and the sides and foundation in bad shape or worse. Projects such as these took more than one season, but much progress was made, including preparing for a permanent metal roof. The dilapidated house soon presented a very different appearance from before.

The old Cumbres snowshed was also in very bad condition. At one time, there were thirteen eight-foot bays, protecting the Cumbres wye from heavy snows in order that trains, locomotives and snowplows could be turned when necessary. In the late 1974, most of the shed collapsed, and later sections of the shed over the switch were removed. There was the very real fear that, like the car inspector's house, both house and shed were doomed. Starting in 1990, however, work on stabilizing the structure commenced and continued in 1991. With the approval of various agencies, especially the state historic preservation offices and the commission, the Friends rebuilt and carefully replaced the first bay.

All of this took careful planning in order to erect a structure estimated to weigh in excess of two thousand pounds. This turned out to be only the first of further extensive repairs and pieces of restoration to be carried out on the Cumbres snowshed in the future. In Chama, the commission contracted to repair and replace an eroded brick wall at the juncture of the old engine house and the newer building. This work required removing a sheet metal shed that enclosed the east wall of the remaining historic engine stalls. The Friends built a new shed that provided a better enclosure for storage, especially during the winter. Section crew bunk cars were rehabilitated inside and received new roofs, roof walks and window frames.

Also, a new piece of historic rolling stock, #55, a thirty-foot (short) refrigerator car, was brought to the property. The car had been discovered at a local airport in Colorado's San Luis Valley, sitting on the ground with all of the metal parts removed. "Reefer" #55 is a long-term project. In other actions, the Chama stock yards were stabilized with wood preservative, the fire hose shed was painted, the stone wall below the loading ramp for the coal tipple was repaired and, finally, landscaping was improved around the yard. Things were simply being made to look better to the visitor. The unsung heroes were the volunteer crews out along the line, painting mileposts and new state line signs. As a result, the volunteers' contribution to the railroad amounted to more than 4,360 hours of restoration work—a valuable contribution for in-kind match for outside funding.

In 1991, two final events occurred in the evolution of the Friends, the railroad and the commission. The commission agreed to an exchange of locomotives with the Durango & Silverton Narrow Gauge Railroad. In exchange for receiving locomotive #482, a K-36 class, the D&S sent over a K-37-class locomotive, #497. The #497 not did run well on the D&S, due to its lines' tighter curvature. The assumption was that it would do well on the C&TS, while the shorter #482 would be better suited to the Durango line. Also that year, Congress appropriated, and President George H.W. Bush authorized, $550,000 for the restoration of locomotive #463, a K-27 class, built by the Baldwin Locomotive Works in 1903. (This appropriation also provided for three new passenger coaches.) As mentioned before, Gene Autry had donated the locomotive to the town of Antonito back in the 1970s that in time sold it to the commission for

The C&TSRR's engine #487 arrives at Sublette with a westbound freight train.

$1, and now the money was in place to restore it to operational condition. Locomotive #463 is one of only two such locomotives still in existence, the other being at the Huckleberry Railroad in Michigan.

That year, 1991, was not all successes or major contributions, for there were also sad tidings. In September, Willis Kyle, president of Kyle Railways, died after a long, debilitating illness. He was succeeded as president by his principal aide, another longtime railroader, Lynn Cecil. W. Earl Bell, a former official of Scenic Railways, also passed away. Bell had been manager of operations on the C&TS in the early 1970s. Another loss was Robert Kurt Ziebarth of Taos, New Mexico. Mr. Ziebarth was a member of New Mexico governor David Cargo's planning staff at the time of the acquisition of the railroad in the late 1960s.

With it all, the future seemed well assured. With an experienced operating company, a growing number of riders (and equally rising income) and an ever-increasing and experienced volunteer movement, all contributed to a rosy outlook.

CHAPTER 8

MORE TO COME

1992 and After

As noted before, 1991 was a banner year for the railroad, the commission, Kyle and the Friends group. Executive Director Leo Schmitz reported that the number of riders increased by 13 percent over the previous year, to a total of 56,037. This number was, of course, a high over any previous year, and he gave credit to Kyle for promoting the C&TS and drawing more riders with an "enjoyable ride with friendly and courteous service." The commission was also involved in several important projects, including renovating several of the Antonito coaches with new windows and interiors while adding insulation to the cars for a quieter ride. Two more of the Antonito cars were due for similar treatment during the winter.

Following a stated practice of not allowing privately owned rolling stock on the railroad, largely due to insurance considerations, the commission proceeded to purchase a caboose, stock car and refrigerator car still owned by some of the Narrow Gauge Railroad group.

The commission also participated in two joint projects with the Friends. One saw the installation of the metal roof on the car inspector's house at Cumbres. The Friends had previously restored the exterior and stabilized the structure, but it was still lacking the metal roof. A second such joint project was to share the cost of rebuilding the Chama roundhouse storage shed, as noted earlier, with a contractor repairing the wall of the old roundhouse in Chama and pouring a new footing. In 1991, the Friends provided the labor of building the new shed. As a result, the total cost of the project was within the commission's budget. The commission also had a long-term plan for the Chama depot, the parking lot, area drainage and the water tank in the Chama yard. These projects, however, had to wait for funding.

The Friends group was also busy with various projects, not the least of which was to locate representative examples of the "missing" oil tank cars. At one time, the Denver & Rio Grande Western owned several dozen such cars. They were converted from standard-gauge cars, which had been built in the first decade of the century, to narrow-gauge between 1924 and 1930. Most of these cars were sold for scrap in 1963. However, sixteen of these narrow-frame, narrow-gauge cars were sold to the White Pass & Yukon Railroad in about 1965 to haul jet fuel for U.S. airbase needs. They were moved to Skagway, Alaska, and remained in service until 1982, when they were taken out of service.

These cars were used primarily to move crude oil from Chama to Alamosa. The crude oil was piped to Chama from the Gramps oil

This double-headed daily train powered by engines #483 and #487 approaches the Cresco water tank for some needed water.

field, fifteen miles northwest of Chama. Oil was first produced there in 1936, and within a short time, there were ten more good wells on a ranch owned by the Hughes family. Their family tradition has the name "Gramps" being derived from the simple explanation that the children referred to their grandfather's property as "Gramps' oil field." Oil was shipped to Chama through a four-inch pipeline, which was partly buried or, alternatively, raised on simple trestles over intervening canyons and arroyos. Just to the west of Chama was a 66,000-barrel storage tank and pump station. Oil was then pumped from this facility to the oil loading rack at the railroad yard. (This rack is still in place.) The oil was then shipped in cars, 150 barrels per car and eight to sixteen tankers at a time, to a refinery in Alamosa. Rail shipments ceased when the refinery was closed in about 1960. These tank cars were sold to the White Pass & Yukon Railroad in 1965. There are twenty-six wells still in operation at the Gramps field. The oil, however, is now sent by truck to Bloomfield, New Mexico.

In 1980, the first contact seeking to return some of the tank cars was made with the White Pass, but nothing much came of it. However, renewed contact was made in 1984, just a year after that railroad suspended operations. (The WP&Y was later revived to carry tourists in part of Alaska and Yukon Territory.) Some money was raised through the Railroad Committee of the Historical Society of New Mexico before the creation of the Friends in 1998. The asking price, however, was unacceptably too high. Efforts continued through 1987, but the result was the same—a price out of our range.

All of this changed in November 1989 when Bill Lock presented a seminar to the Tourist Railroad Association Convention in Denver, Colorado. At that event, C&TS general manager Dan Ranger, also a member of the board of the Friends, introduced Lock to Steve Hites, then manager of Passenger Operations for the White Pass. Hites was born and raised in Colorado and recalled seeing these tank cars in and around Durango, Colorado. He was motivated to help by obtaining a lower price. The White Pass agreed to a price of $7,500 per car delivered to Vancouver, British Columbia—the delivery price alone to Vancouver by sea was $5,000 each! The problems now were negotiating the actual purchase of a certain number of cars from the White Pass & Yukon, arranging funding for that purchase and, finally, setting up transportation.

Dr. Fred Knight, Tank Car Committee chairman, had a job to do. He put in untold hours of phone calls and letters before success. He deserves our thanks for this accomplishment.

One big step came when the Union Tank Car Company in Chicago, the original owner of the cars, came through with a donation. Personal meetings with senior officials of the company in June 1991 resulted in the donation of $22,500 for the purchase of three cars. The Friends group was responsible for transportation and agreed to restore them to their original appearance with UTLX (Union Tank Car Company) markings, as well as to display one in Antonito and two in Chama.

The Friends committee, Bill Lock and Kyle employee Earl Knoob then went back to the White Pass and came to an agreement to buy three cars with an option to purchase additional cars for the same price, up to a total of nine cars. The Friends fundraising activities in 1991, the success of the snowplow charter and the "Moonlight" trains meant that the board could afford to buy one additional car, as well as pay for transportation with other incidental expenses. With that plan in place, Friends member Charles Brown of Camden, Maine, donated $7,500 for the purchase of another car, making five in all. These funds were increased with additional donations from many other members.

In addition, member Randy Worwag of Denver, who was also a volunteer with the Colorado Railroad Museum at Golden, Colorado, ultimately arranged for that museum to buy two more cars from the Friends option. The resulting negotiations by the Tank Car Committee resulted in a package of eight tank cars. The deal was signed on November 1, 1991, with six to the C&TS and two for the museum, with delivery in Alamosa, Colorado.

Before any of that restoration could happen, of course, the cars had to be shipped from north Vancouver to Chama. As noted, the purchase price included transport from Skagway to Vancouver. As the negotiations progressed, Chairman Fred Knight continued to work on the problem. Starting in 1990, he solicited donations of transportation from the mainline railroads involved—at that time, before mergers, this meant the Burlington Northern, Union Pacific and Southern Pacific/Denver & Rio Grande Railroads. There was also the trucking company, Ranger Transport, which was paid by the Friends to transport the cars from north to south Vancouver and to load them on the Burlington flat cars.

Fred Knight spent countless hours by phone and letter in arranging this complicated movement. To his great credit, Fred convinced the Burlington Northern to donate the cost of shipping the cars by rail from south Vancouver to Portland, Oregon; the Union Pacific to donate the cost of shipping from Portland to Salt Lake City; and the Southern Pacific/Denver & Rio Grande Western to donate the cost of shipping them on to Alamosa, Colorado, via Pueblo. The whole project was further complicated by the need to hire a customs broker in order to cross the national borders. On Saturday, February 29, 1992, a dedication ceremony celebrated their arrival. At last, the cars were offloaded in Alamosa onto their trucks on flatbed semi trailers with rails so that the cars could be rolled off the trucks onto C&TS rails at end-of-track in Chama. The two cars belonging to the Colorado Railroad Museum were detached from the train at Pueblo and taken back north to Denver and on to their home at Golden.

After a journey of almost four thousand miles, six of the original UTLX narrow-frame, narrow-gauge tank cars returned to their home tracks. The last car was offloaded at Chama on March 12, 1992. The six cars were restored to their D&RGW configurations, full-size couplers replaced the smaller couplers used by the White Pass, brakes were inspected and repaired and, lastly, a place was prepared along the oil loading dock in Chama. The dock was restored by the Friends for this display. The cars were part of a later freight train special sponsored by the Friends. The UTLX Company was so pleased that it sent a representative to Chama to do an article on the tank cars for *Trans-Action*, the company magazine.

A second valuable collection was added to the growing fleet of historic rolling stock in 1992. Six double-deck stock cars owned by Mr. Carl Helfin, of the Narrow Gauge Motel in Alamosa, were donated to the Friends. Double-deck cars were used for shipping sheep and hogs. The historic stock yards at the south end of the Chama yards were noteworthy in having been constructed to handle both cattle and sheep. Loading ramps were built specifically for either cattle or sheep. The sheep ramps were double deck to make loading of the sheep easier. The lower and upper portions of the stock car were loaded simultaneously.

The Friends group was proving that through perseverance, organization and donations, major developments could be effected to enhance the experience for visitors and riders on the Cumbres line.

While all of this excitement was in progress, the usual work of the Friends and the Railroad Commission continued through 1992. For instance, Osier, Colorado, was always an important place, both in D&RGW days and in more recent times along the San Juan Extension. The lunch stop, with the new dining facility, also serves as the transfer point for passengers going through from one end of the line to the other. The rail yards there were never designed as a tourist orientation. There were passing sidings and, at one time, a turntable for turning locomotives, but the turntable had been removed many years before. Now, in 1992, there was again a need to be able to turn locomotives and even whole trains around.

Again, there were long discussions about where and how to pay for such a new facility. Finally, agreement between all interested parties ended with the plan for a turning loop (rather than a wye) to be built just east of the dinning hall. By that summer of 1992, a grant from the Farmers Home Administration was ready to commit $108,000 for the loop, another siding at Antonito and for bridge ties for the Cascade trestle. Planning began. In August, General Manager Joe Vigil reported that as of August 20, the number of passengers was about 1.5 percent higher than over the same period in 1991. The commission also noted, with great pleasure, the continued work of Friends members during this summer. That

A double-headed C&TS daily excursion train, with #483 on the point, awaits departure while the crew members discuss the situation.

discussion led to a major development between the commission, the Friends and Kyle: the approval of the Triad Agreement.

At the December 4, 1992 meeting of the Railroad Commission, an agreement was signed establishing the Friends as the "official museum support group" for the railroad. This was the Triad Agreement. This document established the legal grounds, practical arrangements, responsibilities for insurance, approval of projects, role of the historic preservation agencies of both states, creation of a permanent Triad Committee, financial responsibility and so forth. There was every reason to be satisfied with this legal document, for it clearly delineated rights and responsibilities of all three parties. Significantly, the Triad Committee has met only a few times to clarify a bit of confusion arising during joint operations, such as special trains sponsored by the Friends. The lack of meetings is a clear tribute to those who drew up the document and the resultant trust among the parties involved.

A second action at that commission meeting was a "Memorandum of Donation" between the Friends and the commission. This was done in light of a recent commission decision that all rolling stock on the property must belong to the commission. This requirement was made in order to provide insurance coverage of the collection without the confusion of privately held cars within the collection. The commission did agree that all such historic restored rolling stock would remain on the "public grounds belonging to the Cumbres & Toltec Scenic Railroad Commission." The Friends group also stipulated that there was "good and sufficient title" and that the donated cars were "free and clear of any liens or encumbrances." The list of donated and restored equipment amounted to fifteen cars, including the two standard-gauge boxcars, the six tank cars, the "short" refrigerator body and the six double-deck stock cars.

In November 1992, a special section of the *Dispatch* summarized the first five years of the Friends. In 1988, the Friends had emerged from the shelter of the Historical Society of New Mexico with 110 members. By 1992, there were 889 from all over the United States, plus 1 from Australia and 3 from Europe. That first work session in 1988 brought 92 volunteers to work in Chama. In 1992, that number grew to 164 volunteers working at five sites along the line. That was only the first five years! By October 1993, the total membership grew to 1,048, with 6 in

Canada, 3 in Australia, 1 in New Zealand, 1 each in Belgium, England and Switzerland and 2 in Germany.

Furthermore, the Friends' financial situation was markedly improved over that first budget report of May 1988, when the balance remaining was $54.00 left from that year's budget of $2,540.00. As of January 1, 1993, income was $56,300.00 and estimated expenses were $59,490.00, leaving a net ending cash of $6,397.68. The Friends group had come a long way and had a long way to go in its programs to support the Cumbres & Toltec Scenic Railroad.

In 1993, the commission was also busy with new projects. The Small Business Administration grant for the restoration of locomotive #463 included enough money for three new passenger coaches. They were already under construction in the Antonito shops and designated as Osier, Cumbres and Sublette. These coaches, seating forty-four passengers, were built on steel frames derived from three standard-gauge flat cars. These frames were sent to Midwest Fabrication and Steel Company in Pueblo, Colorado, to be converted to narrow-gauge configurations. It took between eighteen and twenty operations just to create the component parts before they were welded together. Components for the rest of the cars were built separately and then joined together. Early in 1993, the completed frames were shipped to Antonito for the final assembly. The walkover seats came from old Pennsylvania Railroad coaches.

Later that year, film crews returned from Hollywood to create *Wyatt Earp*. Chama yard was the center of all of this activity. Film companies are always carefully instructed in the treatment of historic cars and buildings, and any alterations were restored to their former configurations. Noted star Kevin Costner spent the night in Chama yard.

The Friends group was also busy. The 1993 summer work sessions brought in 146 volunteers to work at every major site on the line. At Antonito, preparation of a display train continued with carpentry and paint. The buildings at Sublette received much the same treatment, and for the first time, the volunteers labored away at Osier. Work there included moving a spur track back to its original location. Kyle employees then brought a flat car loaded with material from Chama that was parked on the Osier spur. Renovation of the Osier section house roof was begun, the stock pens were surveyed, loose boards all around were renailed and linseed oil for protection was generously applied in preparation for next year. A milestone was reached that summer with the 1000th member of the Friends.

That same summer, an article in the *Dispatch* credited the development of the lunch preparation crew in the Chama yard. Before 1990, noon lunch was a rather pick-up affair. At the first official work session in August 1988, volunteers made their own sandwiches at a table near the engine house. Evening meals were equally do-it-yourself things, with Bill Lock manning the barbecue. Back in the days of the historical society work sessions, it often was "every man for himself" at local restaurants. Then, in 1988, the commission dedicated boxcar #3585 as a lunch and "club" car for the Friends. Dramatic change came in 1990 when modifications and improvements transformed #3585 into a modern food service car. Storage and a sink, with space for a refrigerator, electricity and lights, changed everything. In 1991, a refrigerator was donated and vinyl floors and wall panels added, and finally, in 1992, Formica countertops were added. The Friends finally bought a new refrigerator the same year.

This view of C&TSRR's engine #483 depicts it crossing Los Pinos Trestle with the daily excursion train.

The food served went through a dramatic change as well. In 1990, Friends Betty Schuh and Mary Cardin led a "revolution." Those two were unsatisfied with the quality, content and service provided for Friends crews working from Chama to the most remote places on the line. They changed all of that. By midmorning, individual lunches were on their way to Antonito, Sublette, Osier and Cumbres by road. Later arrangements with the operator had the lunches placed aboard the train for delivery. From 1990 to 1993, the now expanded kitchen crew served three thousand lunches. The lunch crews continue their work to the present with good humor and excellent lunches provided to the volunteers.

The Friends also added another item to the growing list of historic rolling stock when passenger coach #0292 was brought to Chama. The Friends purchased the car for reconstruction and, ultimately, service on the railroad. Jackson and Sharp of Wilmington, Delaware, built car #292 in 1883. After long service and one wreck, #292 was changed into a maintenance of way car for use on the Durango branch. By 1966, the coach was re-lettered "Operation Car 17B" and then re-lettered "Office Car."

That fall of 1993, General Manager Joe Vigil announced that 57,303 passengers had ridden the train. This figure represented a slight drop from the 1992 figure of 58,855 riders. The reasons for this drop were a matter of speculation, from a significant number of people who made reservations but neither paid nor showed up to the recent outbreak of the hantavirus, a sluggish economy and other factors. Vigil pointed out a similar drop on the Durango & Silverton Railroad. Over the winter of 1993–94, the shop crews were kept busy with work on all of the locomotives. This was especially true of the very historic #463, a K-27 class, better known as the "Gene Autry." This is the oldest locomotive on the property, dating from 1903. This locomotive required extensive renovation work, and hopes and plans were for a dedication in 1994.

The new year of 1994 dawned with even more enthusiasm and indications for greater success. On May 6, 1994, the Friends received an award from the New Mexico Historic Preservation Bureau. The occasion was the Twenty-second Annual New Mexico Heritage Preservation Awards ceremony, at which the historic preservation work of nine organizations and individuals was recognized. The Friends received the award "for restoring historic structures and rolling stock on the Railroad." In past years, the railroad itself had been recognized by the National Trust for Historic Preservation; the American Association of Civil Engineers also named the railroad a National Civil Engineering Landmark. This occasion in May, however, was the first recognition for the Friends.

That summer, the C&TS was also the scene of another ceremony. The U.S. Postal Service chose Chama and the rail yard as the location for the "First Day of Issue" of five postage stamps commemorating the development of steam railroad locomotives in the United States in the nineteenth century. Each stamp depicted a famous American-type locomotive built between 1855 and 1893. The first-class stamps (twenty-nine cents) went on sale for the first time in Chama on July 28, 1994.

The festivities included a formal program presided over by Chama postmaster Abigail French, but also present was Allen R. Kane, vice-president of marketing, United States Postal Service, representing Postmaster General Marvin Runyon. Mr. Kane gave the principal address that morning. Also coming to Chama from Washington was Jolene Molitoris, head of the Federal Railroad Administration, and William Withune of the Smithsonian Institution. I represented the Railroad Commission and the Friends Board. Also present were George Lopez, acting Albuquerque district manager of the Postal Service, and James Ozment, retired construction engineer for D&RGW Railroad. Mayor Antonio Gonzales welcomed the participants and audience to Chama. Festivities included booths where, among other things, folks could buy the new stamps, as well as folk art and collectibles. A souvenir program, illustrated by noted railroad artist John Coker, was sold. Other organizations, including the Friends, offered stamped cachets with "Official First Day of Issue" on them. A lot of good fun and publicity resulted for the C&TS and the Friends.

As expected, earlier that spring, locomotive #463 had been dedicated at Antonito. This was done on opening day of the season, making the ceremony doubly festive. There were again booths, welcoming remarks and visiting dignitaries. Nonalcoholic champagne was served, a toast was made and the champagne bottle was broken on the locomotive's smoke box. On June 19, there was another large crowd at Antonito. This was for the dedication ceremony of three new passenger coaches. It was also the inaugural run of #463 to Osier. The run to Osier was also to commemorate the recently completed balloon loop. All in all, it was a wonderful start for the 1994 season on the C&TS.

That same June, the tank car special ran from Chama to Cumbres. There were more than one hundred passengers on the double-headed train. Among the distinguished passengers were three corporate officers from the Union Tank Car Company of Chicago. They came to see the historic cars that had been purchased by the Friends, moved to Chama and restored to operating condition. The Union Tank Car Company had originally built these cars in 1907. The officials were pleased to see the kind of restoration work done by the Friends. President Ken Fischl of UTLX commented, "It is a proud day for both the Union Tank Car Company and the Friends...to have these authentic, original tank cars running exactly the way they did over sixty years ago." The Friends could rightly bask in shared glory with the operator.

That summer was marked by another, and even larger, number of volunteers attending the 1994 work sessions. The projects committee was spending virtually the entire year planning for the coming work sessions. No longer was just a phone call a week or two ahead enough advance planning for a work session. Principal planning was now being done by Bill Lock and Glenden Casteel in coordination with Kyle management in Chama and Leo Schmitz of the commission. Many more volunteers

The Cumbres & Toltec's Rotary Snowplow OM, powered by engine #488, clears the accumulation from the tracks as the train approaches Lobato Trestle.

were involved behind the scenes. Work crews were working in Antonito, Sublette, Osier, Cumbres and the Chama yard. They were renovating buildings and rolling stock and building new facilities, such as the extension of the roundhouse. Whole families were becoming involved in projects. The Smucker family devoted efforts of three generations to the historic coal tipple, describing their work as the "Great Coal Tipple Caper." It was lots of work but fun too! Not only was much being done in 1994, but plans and dates were already announced for 1995 as well.

By November 1994, Lock could announce that membership was now over 1,200, with eight foreign countries represented—Canada, Australia, Japan, Malaysia, New Zealand, Belgium, England and Germany—plus every state in the nation save "poor little Rhode Island." General Manager Joe Vigil could also happily report an increase in the number of riders over 1993—a total of 58,102. In September, Vigil reported that this increase also required more double-headed trains than ever before. Of thirty-one days in July, Kyle had to double-head on twenty-eight of those days. By November, he said that the number of double-headed trains was twenty-five more than in 1993. Chief Mechanical Officer John Bush also reported that five steam locomotives and the diesel were operating. Engine #487 was not in service but would be ready for 1995. Restoration of the Chama water tank was also underway and was expected to be ready for the next season. An important political move transpired in Antonito: the town annexed the railroad yard. This move provided police protection and preferential water rates, an advantageous move for the railroad. Also, an award for the restoration of locomotive #463 was presented by the Tourist Railroad Association. The year closed on a note of triumph for the commission, the Friends, Kyle and the railroad.

In 1995, the spring issue of the *Dispatch* showed new advances in quality and content. Editor Art Nichols announced that this was the eighth year for the publication and that there were to be some changes. Two new columns originated with the spring issue. Many Friends members were model builders, so, for their benefit, "The Modeler's Column," by Ed Walton, was introduced. Also, long-term employee, railroad historian in his own right and modeler Earl Knoob introduced another new column, called "Narrow Gauge Near and Far," as a way to keep Friends informed on other narrow-gauge railroads and developments. Both of these columns continued to make interesting contributions to the newsletter.

Nichols also reported that, henceforth, there would be four issues, to be distributed in the spring, summer, fall and winter, rather than the usual five. Nichols promised more pages in each newsletter, which meant that the *C&TS Dispatch* would include a variety of in-depth, interesting and timely articles. And so, that spring issue contained Walton's and Knoob's columns, as well as the usual information on dates and plans for work sessions, special trains and vignettes of a member of the board of directors.

The board also took up two new initiatives, one long term and the other short term. The long-term project was to plan for a site in Chama at which, with the commission's permission, the Friends would build a new car repair facility. This would mean a structure designed for car restoration, with specialized tools and equipment. This would be a very long-term project since no site was yet selected and funds would have to be raised. On the short term, the Friends decided to expand on the work site in Antonito.

The previous year (1994), the Friends had laid a repair-in-place (RIP) track alongside the older cinder block building—popularly referred to as "Fort Knox." Then the board voted to install heavier electrical service into Fort Knox in order to buy and utilize a commercial power table saw, which required heavy electrical service. Additional work in Fort Knox, including removing much stored "stuff," made the building a much better facility for continued restoration work in Antonito. Kyle Railways employees spent the winter working on all five of the steam operating locomotives. Adding to their labors was the upcoming necessity of attacking the heavy snow. Snowfall, especially late in the season, made this winter almost as great as the winter of 1992–93. On that occasion, it took four days using the rotary to open the line.

So on May 1, Rotary OY, pushed by two engines, left Chama. In an interesting development, and because of potential weight problems in soft spots, two UTLX tank cars (with sturdy frames) were placed between OY and the locomotives. The tank cars had been purchased for a far different reason, but the wisdom of buying them was now very clear. This consist worked up to Hamilton's Point before stopping for the day and returning to Chama. In successive days, work trains were sent out to dump ballast in soft places along the track. Thawing after the snow was removed caused the roadbed to soften.

On May 10, a work train with the regular water car placed between the two engines and OY departed Chama. Near Cumbres Pass, at Coxo, the snow was so heavy and deep that a third locomotive was sent up to help. With the three engines working hard, the entire consist finally made Cumbres at nine o'clock that evening. The next day with two locomotives, the train worked east, but the snow was so heavy they did not reach the Los Pinos area until early evening. Then disaster struck. OY's drive shaft powering the great blade fractured. There was no choice but to return to Chama. The railroad, however, was still not open. There were several large drifts and snow packs remaining on the line.

On May 18, another work train with a pilot plow left Chama with two locomotives—one running backward! Several weeks earlier, a bulldozer had plowed out the Cumbres yard. In the interim, however, a lot more snow had fallen. The backward-running locomotive managed to plow out the yard in order for the train to turn. Then the two engines started toward the east. By noon, they reached Los Pinos siding before running into very deep snow. In two hours of bucking, the engines plowed only 500 of 1,500 feet of heavy snow. At this moment, crew concern for the equipment meant a return to Chama. The next day, an engine with pilot plow departed Chama with a Caterpillar tractor on a flat car. The tractor removed some of the snow, and the crew was confident that remaining drifts could be plowed by the engine. Fat chance! The engine ran into a large section of ice on the rail, and the entire front of the engine was lifted off the track. This was high enough that the locomotive's spring rigging was separated from the running gear. As reported by Knoob, the tractor was fortunately able to push the engine back on the track. The Cat cleared the rest of the track, while the shop crew reassembled the spring rigging. The train returned to Chama at nine o'clock that evening. The rest of the track was cleared by front-end loader.

On May 24, the Antonito train (which had wintered in Chama) with two locomotives, one with the pilot plow, forced their way through narrow cuts and the final drifts, all the way to Antonito. May 27 was opening day! The winters can be rough in the high country of the San Juan Mountains. The work showed how the railroad crews were committed to their jobs and knew what to do without serious incident.

That year, 1995, saw major changes for the Friends. President Bill Lock, founder and president since 1988, stepped down from that office.

Lock was as responsible as any one person for the success of the Friends. He had led the organization from those first few volunteers in those earliest work sessions to the over 1,200 members by 1995. He led the organization to that pinnacle. At the annual meeting in Chama, on July 28, 1995, Lock gave his retirement speech. He had announced the decision to step down before the board of directors meeting the previous summer. He had previously expressed the desire to serve for only another two terms. In the interim, he said, the board had matured and grown and planned for this change.

Now, on July 28, Lock announced that Vice-President Terri Shaw agreed "to serve as President of the Friends of the Cumbres & Toltec Scenic Railroad." He noted her dedication to the organization and her organizational skills: "I believe that Terri is the best person for the job at this time." Lock went on to promise continued active support and involvement in the board and the Friends. The Friends office would continue to be located in his office building in Albuquerque. Now that he was relieved of the presidential chores, he would devote more time to fundraising to support restoration efforts of the group: "I hope you will join me in welcoming Terri and thanking her for taking on what certainly is a most demanding job. Thank you from the bottom of my heart for your support, encouragement, friendship, and love. God bless you."* One of his last acts was to announce that an agreement in principle was reached with Kyle and the commission for the repair facility to be built in Chama.

The Friends' 1995 summer work sessions contributed the usual list of accomplishments from Antonito to Chama. On the east end of the line, the work done at Fort Knox proved that the expenses of new services and equipment for the work there was money well invested. The restoration of the log bunkhouse at Sublette was completed with its painting—chinking between the logs was done earlier. At Osier, crews continued to work on the roof of the section house. Kyle, incidentally, moved carloads of materials to these sites as part of the renovation efforts. The commission paid for a local carpenter to complete the Osier station roof before winter. At Cumbres, extensive work on the car inspector's house returned the building to a condition never dreamed of a few years ago. Painted scenes on the plywood in the windows gave the impression that someone lived there. All that was left for the next year was to raise the building and install a new foundation. In Chama, the usual car painting and lettering, along with continued work on the short refrigerator car, stock pens, surveys and food preparation, were only a few examples of the Friends projects that year.

The commission also reported on its major restoration projects. The Chama water tank restoration was completed. The historic tank had been in dire need, with rotting timbers and the threat of collapse. Several years before, a steel liner was placed in the tank in a "misguided" effort to prevent so much water loss through leaks ("misguided" because the liner then provided only a nearly five-thousand-gallon capacity, and the historic tank was designed to hold fifty thousand gallons, enough to water two locomotives simultaneously through the unique double spouts). This restoration cost $151,436—Colorado and New Mexico each kicked in $32,870, and the commission contributed $85,696. The tank was new construction from the ground up, with the only historic parts reused being the roof and the tie-bands around the barrel of the tank. It was a very useful project, for both preservation purposes and for continued use in support of a booming heritage railway operation.

CHAPTER 9

OPTIMISM AND CHANGE

The winter of 1995 on the railroad was one of continued optimism. The Friends took measures to focus on long-range project planning. In previous years, the main focus of the Friends had been on scraping and painting cars and structures to halt further deterioration. Now the Friends had matured to the point of being able to turn to the kind of projects that would take more than one or even two seasons. Some of the very historic, and seriously deteriorated, cars were candidates for such planning. Cars #053, #054, #065, #0452, #292 and #252 had needs that had to be addressed. A subcommittee of the Friends Board, along with representatives of the operator and the commission, made recommendations to the board. These recommendations were adopted.

The board had to decide what work could be accomplished during regular work sessions and what would have to be done in an enclosed facility. Restoration goals were different for each car, and they had all gone through various changes during their life on the railroad. Car #053 started as a mail/baggage car. It was used later as a cook car for the rotary snowplow. The decision was to retain that later character of the car—crews were still cooking in the car when Kyle ran the snowplow! One of Railway Post Cars #054 and #065 would be restored as an RPO. Car #0452 was scheduled to be restored as a business car. Car #252 would probably be returned as a parlor car and #292 as a coach. For the time being, the cars were covered with tarps to protect them from

The C&TSRR engine #487 leads a double-headed excursion train east of Chama.

the heavy winters. Long-term projects such as these are the driving force behind the move to build a year-round facility.

That spring of 1996, the summer work sessions were also planned. The dates of each work session, for instance, plus major projects for the summer were addressed. Due to the nature of projects for 1996, the board agreed to three weeklong sessions. Inspection car MWO2, for instance, was not in running condition, and Friend Art Randall, who looked at the vehicle last year, hoped to begin its restoration in 1996. Stock cars, "Reefers," the stock pens and Sublette were all among the "usual candidates." Planning for work sessions now took up much more time and effort. Materials, food preparation, distribution of materials and tools in the remote places all required prior organization. The estimates included planning and work for about one hundred members.

There was also a notable amount of work done by Kyle in the shops that winter. The operating locomotives were readied for the annual Federal

A westbound passenger train crosses Cascade Bridge during the winter of 1950 in this photograph by Mike Davis.

Railroad Administration inspection. Other work was scheduled depending on which locomotive needed what work—running gear overhaul for #484, for instance; #497 had come back in service the previous September with new boiler tubes, new front and rear tube sheets, bored pistons and valve cages and new piston and valve rings. Some of this work was necessary in order to store #497 in Antonito for the winter. This left more room in Chama for the others requiring indoor space.

The experience with #463 during the season was a case in point illustrating the difficulties of repair and operation of historic steam engines. The engine developed an unknown steaming problem that required investigation during the winter. In addition, #463 also showed excessive wear on the piston rings after only two seasons. As Kyle employee Earl Knoob explained, #463 had an old-style bolt-together piston made of cast iron. Several pieces were held together with large bolts. One bolt broke during the summer, and the bolt head fell into the cylinder. The piston smashed the bolt head into the front cylinder head, and this bent the piston rod. Knoob said that a new one-piece cast-steel piston would be substituted. There are similar pistons in the #480s. He also noted that the D&RGW knew of the problem and developed a plan for such a replacement piston. This new type had never been implemented, since both remaining locomotives of this type (#463 and #464 in Michigan) still had the old-style pistons. Finally, diesel #15, leased from the Georgetown

Loop Railroad, had two cylinder heads replaced. "As you can see," reported Earl Knoob, "there is always enough to keep us busy."

In preparation for future work sessions, members of the Friends realized that there was no complete compilation of the paint colors and types used since 1988—the first year of the Friends. Also, there was no complete record of which cars and structures were painted in that same period. So, steps were taken by Bill Lock and Art Randall to compile such a record. Art Randall pored over years of paint purchase invoices to match paint colors, formula identification and quantities used with each project. All of this information was added to the rolling stock database in order to create records of when a car or structure had been painted. This record could then be used to evaluate how well the paint job was holding up and anticipate when to paint that item again. Planning for each work session was difficult enough, and now planning was extended over the next several years.

The same lack of a database applied equally to the tools and materials. At the end of work sessions, both tools and leftover materials were dumped, uncounted, into the two boxcars dedicated for that use. For the last two years, 1995–96, volunteers started such a database so that tools and materials could be checked in and out during work sessions. The buying of tools and materials is part of the task for the Project Planning Committee. This new database was a great help in controlling inventory. The Friends continued to refine organization and planning. That summer, the Triad Committee, made up of representatives from all three agencies, met to work out a standardized lettering policy (see *Dispatch*, vol. 9, no. 3, fall of 1996). This was designed to complement the needs of a historic property with the demands of an operating railroad. This was a clear example of collaboration between the operator, the commission and the Friends. For instance, letters of criticism had been received by the commission for placing the logo of the C&TSRR on the restored water tank at Chama rather than the historic logo of the D&RGW. The Triad agreement on the matter was a compromise between using the historic logo on historic rolling stock and buildings versus the modern C&TS logo on operating rolling stock and locomotives. The C&TS logo remained on the rebuilt water tank.

In December 1995, General Manager Joe Vigil announced a 3 percent increase in the number of riders, a total of 59,871, the number in 1994 being 58,102. Riders on the Chama side were almost twice the number from Antonito. This disparity reached almost to capacity for the more modern "green" coaches in Chama. There were times when the number of riders, from Chama, exceeded the capacity of the modern coaches, and the older converted boxcars were pressed into service. As a result, there were some complaints among riders. To offset those who complained about riding in the boxcar coaches, General Manager Vigil instituted a two-price system, with a discount offered for boxcar tickets, and a surprising number of folks realized that a cheaper price was better. Also, he placed plastic cushions, with the railroad logo on them, in the unpadded seats. He figured that if the seats "walked away," the logos were good advertisement!

Vigil also developed a series of variations on the basic trips. Over the years, there were always some passengers who complained that the basic trip was too long. For instance, Antonito travelers could leave the train at Cumbres for a bus returning to Antonito, thus avoiding the last hour downhill into Chama and then the return trip. This option proved to be very popular.

That same year, 1995, the commission also received four grants for two new cars to be built in the Antonito shop. Monies came from USDA/Rural Development, Boettcher Foundation, Gates Foundation and U.S. West Foundation, to the tune of $145,000. Planning for a storm and wastewater detention pond was underway for the Chama yard. Certainly, there was an optimistic outlook for the remainder of 1996 and into 1997. Change, however, was on the way.

On December 1, 1996, Kyle Railways gave up its lease for operation of the railroad. Kyle president Lynn Cecil gave two reasons for this change. First was Cecil's planned retirement by the end of the month. Second, Kyle had just merged with a railroad operator from Dallas, Texas, that had a new focus on regional freight lines. That operator sought more short-line operational possibilities as a result of recent major rail-line mergers with attendant branch line abandonments. The commission advertised for a new operator to take the lease, operate the railroad and then selected a new operator after reviewing several applicants. Those applicants were the Cape Cod, Ohio Central and the Gulf and Ohio Railroads. The chosen operator was the Cape Cod Railway, operated by George Bartholomew, who was involved in several other projects at one time or another. He had participated in the start-up of the Green Mountain in 1964 and operated the Edaville Railroad from 1970 to 1992. Beyond those projects, he started the Cape Cod tourist excursion and dinner trains in 1989, as well as both the Bay Colony and Seminole Gulf (in Florida) freight railroad operations. It appeared that the C&TS was in good hands.

Bartholomew also familiarized himself with the work of the Friends by attending the board of directors meeting in Colorado Springs in November 1996. Along with the board members, he reviewed the results of the work sessions for summer 1996. Those summer sessions were very productive and demonstrated, again, the cooperative spirit of the Triad group. There were 188 volunteers from twenty-eight states and, significantly, New South Wales, Australia. The Friends' reach was visibly widening. In terms of man-hours, the volunteers donated more than 7,500 hours to the railroad. Such figures become important not only as indication of work done but also to serve as an important match to monies for preservation.

Management and employees of the railroad also contributed to the work sessions and, therefore, to the Friends' accomplishments to the historic preservation of the railroad. Friends' tool cars, materials cars and food cars were spotted as requested next to the engine house in Chama. Other cars were moved as needed for painting in the yard. Drop-bottom gondolas were moved to the Friends' repair-in-place (RIP) track in Antonito. Tools and materials were transported by flat car to and from work sites at Cumbres, Osier and Sublette. Kyle Railways, while still operator, loaned a truck to carry shingles to, and remove debris from, the section house roofing project at Cumbres. Kyle track crews helped move crews and materials to remote locations for the replacement of mileposts. Two historic cars were moved onto the property; the one car with trucks was easy, while the other car, without trucks, took a lot more work.

Another Kyle employee drove across the Cumbres Pass to Antonito to weld broken structural members of the gondolas in order for re-decking to proceed. The diesel was placed in position to provide compressed air to borrowed hydraulic jacks so the volunteers could raise the short "Reefer" so crews could work beneath it. A helper locomotive also pulled three sheep cars alongside the reconstructed stock pens to check the clearance—it was perfect. On the final workday, equipment was returned from Cumbres by the most available means: on the tender of the helper locomotive. In many ways, Kyle Railways was a willing partner in the historic preservation of the Cumbres & Toltec Scenic Railroad.

The Friends also established a new department. In 1996, the Friends started a library in the Albuquerque office. Books, magazines, photographs and government documents made up the beginnings of the library collection. The basic concept was to concentrate on narrow-gauge railroads both in the southern Rockies and nationwide (rolling stock, individual narrow-gauge roads, memoirs and historic preservation), as well as a few general railroad and regional histories. Periodicals relating to railroads, modeling, historic preservation and the like were also included. As a result of announcing the creation of a library, a satisfying number of donations and purchases contributed to a growing and increasingly useful library. In short order, the library also became an archive of original materials. Some archival donations were of museum quality, hence the institution became a library/archive/museum. The Friends also established a website in order to reach out to members and potential supporters. This was a very active development.

To top off a very interesting and changing year, the Friends received another prestigious award. This time, the award came from the Colorado Historical Society, a state agency, at the society's 117th Annual Meeting, December 12, 1996. The citation read: "In recognition of outstanding achievement in preserving Colorado's cultural heritage."*

The autumn issue of the *Dispatch* was usually devoted to a summary of the previous work sessions and an update of planned winter work on the locomotives. In the spring issue of 1997, President Terri Shaw enumerated the Friends' contributions, starting with thanks to the members who do so much for the railroad. As she noted, Friends members contributed in many ways: by the purchase of cars for the collection, by the purchase of tools and materials for work projects and by the value of Friends labor, all adding to the value of the historic collection of locomotives, cars and buildings. She pointed out that about three-fourths of total revenue was spent on Friends programs, about half on restoration and the other half on education and interpretation. In the eight years since its establishment, the Friends had invested about $94,000 to add eighteen historic cars to the property. At the same time, the Friends spent almost $200,000 on the summer work programs. The value of contributed labor was at least $500,000.

The C&TSRR engine #488, with a simulated work train, is waiting in the hole to meet #484 with the daily excursion train.

In the past, the operator had contributed to the railroad by maintaining rolling stock and right-of-way, plus joint funding of long-term projects with the Railroad Commission. The maintenance of rolling stock cost about 30 percent of the operator's budget. Tie replacement cost at least $70,000, with an average of 2,500 ties per year.

The Railroad Commission also contributed by finding the funds for wide-ranging capital improvements—tourist-related projects including new cars, new restrooms and restoration of equipment, such as #463 and Rotary OY. Other funds were found for the right-of-way improvements, including Cascade Creek Bridge and Chama River Bridge and even the Chama water tank. In the eight years between 1988 and 1996, the commission had raised $2.2 million to invest in the property, and about half of that was from grants. Of those grants, in five years almost $78,000 came from Colorado gaming funds. Those funds were combined with the Friends' in-kind labor to make possible the work on the section houses at Osier and Cumbres.

All of this was only a beginning, as needs for future improvements continued. There will always be more work, as wooden bodies and buildings continue to weather. Future projects will always have to call on further contributions to support the Friends and their work.

The new operator, George Bartholomew and his chief mechanical officer, Jack Campbell, detailed work for the shop during the winter. The fall of 1996 was time for transition to the new operator, and that process required considerable time for inventory of supplies, parts, tools and so forth. That process delayed the winter shop program somewhat. Nevertheless, Campbell began an aggressive program for the locomotives. He began to rearrange the machine shop for more effective use of the space. He dreamed of the shop becoming self-sufficient. Up to now, some locomotive work—wheelwork, for instance—had to be sent to the Durango & Silverton shops for work. All in all, things seemed to be progressing nicely.

By the summer of 1997, there were several developments of considerable interest. The Friends developed a new satellite facility at the Western Museum of Mining and Industry just north of Colorado Springs, Colorado. That museum has developed into a premier institution with valuable examples of mining machinery, as well as mining exhibitions (with the machines operating on compressed air). The museum was receptive to railroad-related activity as complementing the museum collections. It was also interested in attracting more of its own in-house volunteers. A collaborative agreement would serve both ends and both organizations. For the Friends, it meant carrying on car restorations year round in a former dairy barn situated on the museum grounds. This also meant a facility close to the nearly two hundred Friends members living in the Denver, Colorado Springs and Pueblo areas. The plan was for a car to be transported to the museum, restored and returned to the C&TS. As one car was sent back to Chama or Antonito, another went back on the same truck to Colorado Springs. Both the commission and the operator applauded the project. So, the first car, pipe gondola #9558, was moved to WMMI for restoration from the frame up.

Secondly, reported President Shaw, the Friends' plans for an enclosed work facility in Chama was progressing. At the March 1997 board of directors meeting, plans and cost projections were presented. Also at that meeting, Chief Mechanical Officer Campbell proposed a project to replicate roundhouse stalls on the site of the historic roundhouse in the Chama yard. Only two stalls remained of the original nine-stall brick roundhouse built at the turn of the century. An original wooden roundhouse burned down in the fire of 1898 that destroyed a lot of the railroad and town structures. Shaw noted that when the "new" engine house was built in 1977–78, there were only two operable steam locomotives of the nine that were purchased from the D&RGW originally in 1970. By 1997, there were six operable steam locomotives, plus Rotary Snowplow OY. Enclosed space was needed, and replication would serve to return the yard to an earlier appearance. Of course, a roundhouse needs a turntable.

The commission was aware of such a turntable being available in Denver. That summer, the commission acquired a historic turntable from Elitch Gardens, a Denver amusement park, that had originally belonged to the Colorado & Southern Railroad. For the price of shipping, the structure was moved to the Chama yards. The previous owner had used the roundtable for both standard- and narrow-gauge operations. Some questions were raised, however, as to the propriety of incorporating a 100-foot through truss bridge turntable, which was not at all compatible with the 65–75-foot, flat girder turntables traditionally used by the D&RGW. The C&S structure is built like a bridge, with trusses as tall as the historic roundhouse. Later conversations with the Historic Preservation Bureau in Santa Fe proved this concern to be correct—a through truss type was not acceptable. The D&RGW used a bridge-girder type of turntable throughout its narrow gauge system, and the last one in Chama was only 65 feet long, versus the 102 feet of the C&S one. (It was not installed, and there are hopes that another railroad will take the turntable away.)

The summer work sessions attracted 150 people. Projects extended all along the sixty-four miles of narrow-gauge line, including the rehabilitation of structures in Chama, rolling stock, Cumbres section house, the Osier section house and depot and window coverings at Sublette. At Antonito, cement pads were poured along the RIP track, and all of that was done in June. There was much more accomplished in August. The commission, operator and Friends group shared in rehabilitating the sand house roof, and new supports for the sand tower were a part of that project.

That August in Antonito, the Friends started a two-year project. With help from the regular track crews, they began installing parts of the three-rail switch on new ties at the west end of the dual-gauge display track. The switch had come from the power company yard in Alamosa.

Three-rail switches are now extremely rare and made it possible for both narrow- and standard-gauge cars and locomotives to operate at the same time and in the same consist. This project was due for completion in 1998. This display complemented the dual-gauge display.

In 1998, the Friends group celebrated its first ten years. At the fall board meeting, President Shaw asked the assembled members to take glory in the past and try to see the future. She recalled past accomplishments by referring to the quality of the newsletter and the "outstanding website," as well as the dramatic changes at Cumbres Pass, the restoration of Sublette village and the cars purchased and returned to the railroad. It was noted that it was hard to measure the mission and commitment to the work of the Friends by its worldwide membership, yet the cash donations and donated labor give strong indications of that dedication. All the directors recognized the essential cooperation among the three entities represented in the Triad—the commission, the operator and the Friends. Diverse talents and professionalism were mentioned, along with camaraderie and friendships developed over the years.

In conjunction with the operator, discussions ranged far and wide on the attractions of the C&TS and how to improve the property for the visitor. Riders come to the railroad for many and diverse reasons. Some come to see and hear live steam locomotives on narrow-gauge rails. Others come to see the scenic landscapes, to experience and feel the history of the West or to see a railroad yard as it was sometime in the 1920s. Directors agreed with the operator that this railroad was already a world-class living history museum. Directors offered ideas of how to further improve that experience, with demonstrations of equipment, such as operation of the coal tipple and maintenance of way rolling stock. There was agreement that the Friends group needed to increase its activities in communicating the special nature of the place to casual visitors, who knew little, if anything, about railroad history.

The need to communicate with the visitors was acted on that summer (1998). Howard Bunte started a program of addressing the riders in each car before departure from Chama. He explained a bit of the history of the line, of narrow gauge and of why the railroad was built in the first place and also answered questions. By midsummer, a second Friend had joined in the fun, and fun it was. Riders responded with enthusiasm, even giving cash donations for the work of the Friends. Bunte and other

"Train Hosts" continued to meet casual visitors at the yard for the rest of the day. There were very interesting chats with folks who did not know of the C&TS, who just happened to drive past. Also of interest were the numbers of European travelers, some of whom spoke almost no English. In time, these volunteers would be known as "Train Hosts," with distinctive aprons having pockets for free literature.

The members went on to dream of an indoor facility for long-term restoration projects. A final site plan was being prepared, as well as drawings prepared and fundraising ideas conceived. The turntable and roundhouse were considered viable joint projects, but all the Friends members realized that such projects must conform to the standards set by state and federal historic preservation agencies.

That summer of 1998, the New Mexico Office of Cultural Affairs, Historic Preservation Bureau, again honored the Friends with the Heritage Preservation Award. The award praised the Friends group for "continuing involvement in the preservation, enhancement and interpretation of the historic railroad between Chama, New Mexico, and Antonito, Colorado." This was the second such award given to the Friends by the same agency. The first was in 1994.

Another award that came to the Friends group was financial in nature. The Wild Oats Community Markets of New Mexico, one of the leading purveyors of organic foods in the country, selected a nonprofit organization to participate in a "five percent day." This amounted to 5 percent of gross sales from all five Wild Oats Markets in New Mexico at the time—two in Albuquerque and three in Santa Fe. In exchange, Friends members were allowed to man tables in each of the five stores, with volunteers handing out materials and talking to interested patrons of the stores. On Tuesday, March 17, 1998, volunteers spent the day, late into the evening, handing out pamphlets for the Friends and the railroad. Bartholomew offered ten pairs of complimentary tickets for the 1998 season. The Friends members awarded these as prizes to shoppers at the Wild Oats stores. The reward came a few days later in the form of a check to the Friends for $6,243.15 for historic preservation expenses. It was a fitting tribute to the Friends organization, being selected over other applicants, to say nothing of the profit.

That spring, the commission also reported on various upcoming projects, such as the waste water system at Chama, a Colorado gaming grant of $69,206 for restoration work on the Cumbres and Osier section houses and construction of a new foundation under the Osier depot. Projects such as these increased collaboration between the commission and the Friends group, with the former providing additional funds in exchange for Friends providing labor. It was (and is) a good way to stretch the money. Leo Schmitz also reported on new incoming money for five ADA (American with Disabilities Act) projects. As required by law, new construction must be accessible for those with disabilities. These structures to be remodeled were the Antonito depot, the commission office in Antonito, the Antonito car shop, the Osier facilities and the Chama engine house/shop and site. Schmitz also noted, in response to a question about planning, that back in 1994 the Friends had been involved in the capital improvement plan that year. He noted also that this was a continuing process, especially in matters of historic preservation, and that the Friends played a vital role.

In that first ten years, under the leadership of Lock and Shaw, the Friends group matured into a proven, experienced, demonstrably effective organization. The combination of awards in historic preservation, the capability to raise the kinds of funds required to purchase and transport historic equipment and a well-presented and erudite newsletter with a capacity to reach out to the general public had, in the process, created a dedicated and growing membership. All of this now placed the Friends group in the top ranks of the volunteer railroad preservation movement, nationwide and worldwide.

This move toward preservation of historic railroads, structures and equipment developed over several decades throughout the industrial world. Effective new organizations appeared devoted to the general topic of railroad history. Museums such as the Colorado Railroad Museum—a private, nonprofit organization—joined with state programs such as the Pennsylvania Railroad Museum, which developed programs to preserve, protect and/or operate vintage railroad equipment. The association of historic preservation with historic operating railroads attracted the visiting public in ever-increasing numbers. Numbers meant increased revenue, which led to developing more programs.

This marriage of tourism with historic operating railroads was a boon to these various projects. The tourist aspect led to the creation of organizations such as TRAIN (Tourist Railroad Association) and ARM (the Association of Railway Museums). Regular railway magazines, such as *Trains* and *Railfan & Railroad*, produced more articles devoted to historic projects. For ten years, one such journal was devoted entirely to historic preservation; unfortunately, *Locomotive & Railway Preservation* did not last beyond its tenth birthday. These few examples only substantiate the growth of the entire railroad preservation movement, and Friends members were now playing in the big leagues.

In 1998, President Terri Shaw was elected to the board of ARM. At the fall meeting of ARM, President Shaw delivered a detailed account of just how the Friends group organized its work sessions. Her talk was entitled, "Volunteering on a Grande Scale: The Friends of the Cumbres & Toltec Work Sessions."* Editor Aaron Issacs started off by remarking that this was "something unprecedented in the railway museum movement." He noted that "[v]olunteers are being recruited and deployed on a scale never before seen." There are so many volunteers that difficult and long-term projects are done "in days what many would expect to take months or even years." This was a "new model for running a restoration program, something the entire industry should take note of."

Therefore, when President Shaw was scheduled for a seminar at the 1998 ARM Convention, Issacs virtually quoted her address. He began by recapping the background of the two states' purchase of the railroad and the early volunteer work. As noted here and by Issacs, conflict between operator and volunteers ended that first group's activities. As also noted in these pages, a new volunteer movement emerged in 1981, was formalized in 1982 and had become the Friends by 1988. Shaw went on, as reported by Issacs, to show how the detailed planning and the utilization of increased focused manpower have led to projects being completed in days or weeks. She acknowledged that there are multiyear projects on the railroad but that proper use of manpower "dramatically reduces the 'drudgery factor' so that a volunteer sees real progress in a short time." This is done in two ways. One way is to marshal overwhelming force to do that "drudge" work, and another is to organize special functions at the end of the session as rewards—barbecues, dinners and train rides. Issac editorialized, "The people who can stick it out through this [drudge] phase are few and probably sainthood material."

The work sessions were directed by two entities authorized by the board of directors. These are the Project Planning Committee and

Administration & Support Committee. The Project Planning Committee is made up of four task group leaders, site project managers and selected others. Project Planning directs team leaders in matters relating to projects, tools, materials and manpower needs. This committee also deals with the railroad's chief mechanical officer on mechanical projects. The members also order tools and materials and schedule delivery of such to work sites. Finally, this committee prepares submissions to the state historic preservation offices for prior approval before work actually begins. Administration & Support deals with registration, meals, chroniclers (who record the work done) and management of the database.

Team leaders acted as "sergeants," or supervisors, at each work site. They started early on, helping to select projects and develop details of the work at their site. Their input determines the materials, tools and manpower needed. A draft of each work plan was submitted three months beforehand. The team leader was responsible to the site leader for adjusting matters in order that work was completed as planned. There was a daily chore of cleaning up the site and storing tools and materials. Upon completion of a work session, each team leader submits a report to the Project Planning Committee for the September meeting. All such reports were bound and sent on to the commission, operator and the Friends library. Planning for the following year started before the end of the work sessions in August. A formal meeting of the Project Planning Committee came in September. From September on, a series of steps summarized the work session and began the formalized planning for the coming year.

There was no official log of the hours contributed by the Friends in any one year. Shaw estimated, however, that taking into account all of the work done in planning, preparation and actual work done, the Friends in 1998 amassed 10,700 volunteer hours. This meant, wrote Issacs, that one hour of preparation, coordination and supervision resulted in four worker hours. Shaw went on to say that communication was the foundation for such successes. "Planning at its most basic is a group of people talking to each other about what they would like to accomplish and how to achieve it…It takes a lot of time, but…it is well spent and the results satisfying." Issacs advised those who missed the speech to write to President Shaw. It was a great compliment, of course, to all who went before up to that moment. There was more to come, however, as relations between the commission and the operator will soon worsen.

Chapter 10
Ups and Downs and Ups

Just as President Shaw was speaking to the ARM convention on the plans and practices relating to the work sessions, former president Bill Lock wrote a retrospective on the last ten years. Lock included in his review of accomplishments the work done before the incorporation of the Friends in 1988. He believed the restoration work fell into certain "pattern and themes." For instance, the dominant theme during the 1980s was that of car painting. The very extensive collection of narrow-gauge freight rolling stock had, with few exceptions, not been painted nor maintained since 1948. That year saw a general repainting of the rolling stock in the Alamosa yards.

In the 1950s, the D&RGW emphasized carrying pipe for the oil and gas fields in northwestern New Mexico at the expense of the remaining rolling stock. In the 1960s the freight business on the narrow gauge dried up, which meant that there were no funds for maintenance. The same lack of funds for maintenance was true during the first decade of the C&TS, except for those few cars painted by the Narrow Gauge Railroad Association. During the 1980s, Lock pointed out, the new volunteers painted more than fifty boxcars, gondolas, stock cars and refrigerator cars plus did maintenance on these same cars. In those same years, the volunteers painted several display engines and restored two maintenance of way cars that were fire damaged. Lock referred to that job as a "confidence builder for the future."

It was a noteworthy event when then project chairman Glenden Casteel reported in 1989 that major repainting was done and that the organization needed to move on to other projects. In the next two years, one work session moved out of the rail yards to the entire town of Sublette. Starting in 1991 and continuing for the next six years, Friends members restored the entire town—new roofs, repairs to siding and painting. That project, thought Lock, indicated that "if…the '80s could be viewed as the decade of car painting, the '90s can be viewed as the decade of structures" repair. The section houses at Osier and Cumbres, with a total rebuild of the dilapidated car inspector's house at Cumbres, also received heavy injections of volunteer labor. One of the most dramatic restorations occurred in saving the twelve bays of the Cumbres snowshed. That job required major structural work to be done, using historic hand methods and techniques. These restoration projects were accomplished in careful cooperation with the historic preservation offices of both states, and in time, we were recognized for such.

Along with these physical accomplishments, ongoing efforts to interpret the historic property to the increasing thousands of visitors continued. One of the earliest projects, in 1984, was to print a walking tour brochure for both Chama and Antonito. The brochure was accompanied by video monitors in both depots and, of course, the evolution of the *Dispatch*. Public enthusiasm was always generated through special charter trains, usually sponsored by the Friends group. Finally, Lock referred to the historic rail cars added to the collection during the 1980s—tank cars, stock cars, historic passenger cars and the short "Reefer." The dual-gauge display in Antonito was also a significant contribution. All of this activity contributed to a hallmark of craftsmanship, good fun and fellowship, which meant the continued growth of the Friends.

It is also very important to note that in all public pronouncements and printed releases, the Friends assiduously emphasized that the volunteers were in no way engaged in, nor responsible for, operating the trains. All operations of locomotives and trains were within the sole responsibility of the operator. The operator held the exclusive right to operate trains through a contract with the Railroad Commission. There was absolutely no thought among the members of the board and the general membership that the Friends group would or should operate trains. It is rather commonly misunderstood in the eyes of the general public that the Friends group was somehow responsible for operations and, even more oddly, that members were paid salaries and expenses for attending work sessions. The latter was certainly untrue, and the former, concerning operations, was about to change.

In late 1996, George Bartholomew was awarded the contract by the commission to operate trains starting in 1997. At the end of that first year, Bartholomew announced a dramatic increase in numbers of riders from more than fifty-four thousand to more than sixty thousand. He and his chief mechanical officer also announced ambitious plans for the coming 1998 season. There were, however, disquieting reports beginning to circulate of troubles within his company. Rumors and talk of lack of track and right-of-way maintenance and deferred work on passenger cars and, most importantly, on locomotives began to surface. Supposedly, major parts were removed from out-of-service locomotives—parts destined for one engine being diverted to another and so forth. This kind of talk was heard during and after the 1998 work sessions by various members of the Friends group, thus giving rise to privately held concerns. Stories of unpaid bills, lack of overtime for employees used in maintaining operating locomotives and the like continued on into the remainder of that season.

A major blow to the operator's credibility came in the spring of 1999. During that fall and winter, the Friends group planned another special fan trip before the regular season opening. This was a two-day affair in April, from Antonito to Osier and the return. The second day was also a fan adventure in conjunction with opening the track. It had been a very mild winter in the high country that year. There was perhaps only two or three feet of snow at Cumbres Pass rather than the more usual twenty-foot drifts associated with "normal" winters there. The first day's round trip went off without a problem. The second day, with two locomotives and a flanger between the first and second locomotive, went uneventfully until just west of the Los Pinos water tank (milepost 325.60). There was some new snow, a few inches covering the tracks, as the train worked uphill toward Cumbres Pass. At that point, lead locomotive #484 rolled up on ice hidden by the new snow, went up and off the rails, coming to rest on the ground, tilted on the left side at a forty-five-degree angle. There were no injuries.

The location was a little-used ranch road, and the snow was packed into ice in the crossing. The effect of thaw and freezing created the ice that derailed the locomotive. The new snow covered the crossing, hiding the problem from the crew of #484. The accident occurred on April 25. The locomotive was not rerailed until May 13, the day before opening of the regular season. The approximate quarter mile of dirt ranch road required reinforcing until two 120-ton cranes could reach the site to lift the locomotive back onto the rails. After inspection and lubrication of running gear, #484 was towed to Cumbres and later returned to Chama. Indeed, on opening day, the regular train was delayed about an hour while #484 was towed to Los Pinos siding in order for the regular train to continue on toward Osier. The locomotive was not returned to service that year and was restored to service for the 2001 season.

In the meantime, planning continued for the coming work sessions and for a new program of "train hosts." This program had begun in 1997, with only a few hosts working the crowds before train time. In 1998, the program expanded to hosts riding the trains from both ends of the line. The experiences of these hosts revealed a considerable problem for the volunteers. Trying to talk over the noise of the train was proving to be a bit hard on one's vocal cords. Friends member Lee Ritterbush drew on his considerable audio engineering background to provide a solution. His solution not only would be of help to the volunteers but also would serve the conductor and, therefore, the riders. The conductors were using a very inadequate sound system to communicate with the passengers, with a message of welcome, safety and general instructions.

On September 2, 1998, Lee submitted a very detailed report to the Friends Board of Directors recommending a whole new audio system for both the Chama and Antonito trains. The upshot of his work came at the December meeting of the Railroad Commission. The commission and the operator agreed to fund the project, with the Friends providing the labor over a two-year period. These new systems were designed to benefit both the train conductors and our riders. The host would use the same car speaker system as the conductor, but the two would not conflict. There was another major benefit to the Friends' participation in the program. In investigating the requirements of the Federal Disabilities Act as applied to various Friends' programs (walking tour brochures, for example), this system would satisfy the obligation of the Friends, the Railroad Commission and the operator to do as much as possible to "interpret the railroad to visually handicapped riders." The program continued to grow into the 1999 season.

On an upbeat note, that spring the Friends group was again honored. During the regular session of the New Mexico legislature, the House voted a memorial in honor of the Friends. The memorial "recognized and commended" the Friends group "for their many contributions that have been vital to the preservation and promotion of the Cumbres & Toltec Scenic Railroad." Not only were the Friends honored, so, too, was the railroad. The Society of International Railways Travelers named the C&TS as one of the World's 20 Best Rail Trips. These honors were perhaps even more important than anyone at the moment realized in the light of coming events.

That summer, starting with the spring derailment, there was a perceived deterioration of the roadbed and equipment. Knowledgeable members of the Friends had expressed some misgivings even the year before. Now, in this new season, there were more shortcomings apparent to many. Rumors of unpaid bills, termination of city services at one time, delayed train departures because of the need to change brake shoes and the like began to surface with increasing frequency. Friends' work, however, continued on through the summer season. The list of projects, short and long term, was very impressive as usual. The pile driver OB was moved from Chama to the Friends' facility at the Western Museum of Mining and Industry north of Colorado Springs. A host of other projects from Chama, along the line, to Antonito were addressed in two work sessions in June and one miniature session in May by 176 volunteers. That does not include the two work sessions in August.

The fall issue of the *Dispatch*, however, carried other, more doleful news. Two very valuable and notable members of the Friends group passed away. Director Ralph Flowers joined the organization in 1991 and soon became both a team leader and member of the board of directors. He was killed in an airplane crash on September 1. The loss of Ralph's leadership and knowledge was a great one. On August 20, Friends member Mike Hipskind died of a heart attack at Cresco Tank while photographing the Chama train. His enthusiasm and generosity also meant a great loss for the Friends. Leadership, knowledge and generosity are key elements in the makeup of our membership.

That same fall issue also reported on the increasing concern of the Railroad Commission over the condition of the operating locomotives and the track. At a regular meeting in September, the commission concluded that the C&TS Corporation (Bartholomew) had not responded to concerns raised during the current season. At the September 14 meeting, the commission terminated the operating lease. This action was prompted mainly due to the lack of care "for the historic assets of the railroad and the continued employment of local residents." The commission called for an audit of the C&TS Corporation and then voted to terminate the lease. Backed by advice from the Colorado attorney general, notice was served on the corporation alleging breaches of contract, which, if the audit was not done within thirty days, permitted the termination of the lease.

The list of problems cited were many: 1998 financial statements seemed to show that the corporation's debts exceeded its assets by "a substantial amount." The commission concluded that the corporation was not "financially responsible or capable to operate the railroad." Required financial statements were six months late and submitted only after the commission demanded them. When Bartholomew took over in 1997, there were six working steam locomotives and the diesel in operation. Now there were only three steam locomotives and no diesels working in operation, and the three were in poor condition and in need of major repair. The other three locomotives were out of service, and there were no material plans in place to repair them.

The operator, the list went on, failed to install the "required" 2,500 ties per year for 1998 and 1999. Rent payments, current in September 1999, were made late in two months of 1998 and three months of 1999. Finally, former operator Kyle Railways had left many spare parts and tools, as well as expendable supplies, but they were depleted and needed to be inventoried and replaced. Back in July, the commission contracted with a California corporation, CalShay & Associates, to inspect the steam locomotives of the C&TSRR. A formal agreement was reached on July 22, and the inspection was conducted from August 16 through August 21. Dan Ranger and Steven M. Butler of CalShay carried out the inspection. Ranger was the former general manager of the C&TS when Kyle Railways was the operator.

The CalShay report referred to the Federal Locomotive Inspection Law(s) first passed in 1911, as well as more recent revisions, which were designed to make certain that steam locomotives were operated in "safe and suitable manner." It pointed out that these federal rules of maintaining locomotives were *minimum conditions*. "Every operator," it noted, "should *never* allow their equipment to fall below [these] requirements." It concluded that each of the operating locomotives could "be brought to a safe and reliable service condition," if resources in manpower and funds were made available. Ranger and Butler also made pointed remarks concerning Bartholomew's previous public statements, charging that "previous operators did not do an adequate job in maintaining the equipment"—a charge strongly denied by Ranger. He noted that when Kyle left the property there were five "reliable" locomotives. A sixth (#488) was awaiting boiler work with the necessary tubes and flues on hand, which were newly purchased by Kyle before leaving—"not an act of someone trying to cut repair expenses," wrote Ranger. The CalShay report also included the maintenance program for 1989–96 by Kyle chief mechanical officer John Bush.

In September, Chief Mechanical Officer Walter Rosenberger responded to the CalShay report in a letter to Leo Schmitz of the commission. "While I have taken numerous exceptions to their report," he wrote, "as a whole I feel it is a reasonable accurate document." He agreed that the locomotives needed "significant repairs."

Rosenberger started by questioning whether or not the commission had complied with the open meeting laws in awarding the contract to CalShay. Rosenberger alleged that CalShay had not asked for certain programs that were available, "our maintenance program," for instance. "I do have a maintenance program that recognizes the deficiencies of our locomotives," the federal rules "notwithstanding." The ultimate goal was to have engines in such good condition "that the majority of maintenance is preventative." The real point, he wrote, was reliable locomotives to pull passenger coaches, and not "Grade B" maintenance. CalShay had compared the federal rules to "grade achievement" with letter grades A through D. The federal rules, as noted here, were minimum, or a grade of D or D-. The operator should strive for a grade of B or better, said Ranger.

Rosenberger derided letter grades as meaningless for "railroaders," likening such to a "restaurant sanitation rating." He went on for three pages, in great detail, regarding each locomotive and an action plan for addressing problems. Rosenberger noted that when he arrived on the property in August 1998, he found that the maintenance program "had deteriorated to an 'as needed' or 'crisis' basis." He also referred to the lack of information of maintenance from previous operator files.

(There was no chief mechanical officer for most of 1998. Rosenberger's predecessor had quit for personal reasons.) Again, the charge was often repeated that summer, which was of the "previous operator's [Kyle's]" dereliction of duty. In conclusion, Rosenberger "enjoyed" the relationship with CalShay. That company was not, he noted, "an impediment to our normal operations." He hoped that this "second opinion" would permit the commission and operator to "move forward."

At the September meeting, where C&TS Corporation was given notice of termination, Bartholomew spoke of many problems that year, which started with the derailment of #484. The commissioners, however, continued to express doubts about his ability to take care of the railroad's historic assets and to continue to provide jobs. Two Colorado commissioners, Lewis Entz and Wayne Quinlan, spoke of a downward spiral in the "health" of the railroad to the point of fearing that the railroad would not run in the year 2000. Bartholomew noted that there was a difference of interpretation over "capital improvements" and "general maintenance." According to the lease, the operator was responsible for general maintenance. He asserted that many of the locomotives had problems that extended back for fifteen or twenty years. The commissioners were positive, however, that the railroad would run the next year. Friends members determined to maintain their working relations with both the commission and the operator.

Criticisms continued to mount. Stories were noted of passengers being turned away due to the lack of cars, caused, it was alleged, by the lack of locomotives. Locomotive engineers requested, informally, their legal obligations and rights when required to operate locomotives they regarded as being in dire need of repairs. There were continuing stories of unpaid bills due from the operator and the like.

In September, the commission deferred any further action until October and the end of the regular season. This action obviated the possibility that the riding public would conclude that the trains had stopped running in September. The fall color season is one of the busier times on the C&TS and therefore very profitable for the railroad. Also, this was to give Bartholomew time to clear up all enumerated deficiencies with regard to tie replacement, locomotive work and so forth. On October 19, however, the commission met again in Chama. There were other meetings before October 19, but no public action was taken. These latter meetings were primarily in closed sessions in order to confer with representatives of both states' attorneys general. The October meeting attracted a very large and vocal crowd.

The meeting started with a four-page "Statement and Press Release" by Mr. Bartholomew. He blamed the commission for inaccurate statements "regarding the condition of the steam locomotives." The locomotives, he said, "are in need of major capital repairs." In this context, "capital repairs" meant that the commission was responsible for funding them. The current contract, as well as those of previous operators, always made a distinction between "capital" and "maintenance." By asserting that the locomotives needed "to be rebuilt from the ground up," he moved the locomotives into the capital expenditures column, a clear commission responsibility and a move that the commission firmly denied.

Bartholomew then went on to attempt the same shifting of responsibility of track maintenance. Locomotives and track, he said, are part of a "symbiotic relationship." When one was in need of repair, it was hard on the other. Therefore, there was the need for an "aggressive locomotive and track rebuilding program, requiring substantial outlay of capital funds." Again the reference to "capital" was the key element. This was not a "mis-management" problem, and the problems would not "go away with a change in operators." This was a matter of "resource allocation" and was the "Commission's sole responsibility."

The C&TSRR Corporation, he asserted, was not responsible for capital improvements either "legally or morally." His corporation could not go on year after year losing money while hoping to be reimbursed by the commission. This situation had gone on for three years, he said, and could not continue. The commission's threat to terminate the contract only served to drive away potential investors and "created fear and panic among our creditors." He claimed that suppliers stopped allowing thirty days to pay and began to demand cash on delivery. This last statement flies in the face of accounts of unpaid bills due long before the current crisis. The Friends group's office in Albuquerque received a number of requests for payment when, in fact, the organization was not the party responsible for those unpaid bills contracted by Bartholomew and his C&TSRR Corporation. The bus company went unpaid, as did several other suppliers. New brake shoes arrived only on the opening day of 1996, delaying the departure of the train.

Bartholomew denied that the commission had the legal authority to audit the corporation's books. He offered the commission a look at the books, but only if they agreed to "sign a confidentiality agreement first." It was only because of his warning to the commission about lost revenues for the motels in Chama and Antonito that prompted the commission to extend the October 16 deadline to the October 19 meeting. Extending the deadline permitted the operator to begin a winterizing program "in order to protect and safeguard the priceless and irreplaceable locomotives and other assets." The commission paid to have the locomotives winterized and prepared for federal inspection. Bartholomew brought up the possibility of another corporation buying out his company to run the railroad. Individuals from Alamosa, Colorado, were present to represent this other group. They attempted a presentation before the commission but were unable to show any financial background. The commissioners' motion to accept their proposal failed due to the lack of a second. Bartholomew's contract was terminated on October 19, due to breach of contract.

For the record, Executive Director Leo Schmitz reported that 1,591 ties were installed in 1999; these, however, were supposed to have been installed the previous year. Therefore, C&TS Corporation was still short 605 ties in 1998, as well as 2,500 ties for 1999. On the basis of this as well as other criteria, Leo Schmitz was directed to "take possession of the property" and prepare for federal inspection. He was also directed to begin the process of looking for another operator.

Commission chairman Medardo Sanchez then asked for one hour of public comment from the roughly 150 people present. The intensity of these comments revealed the depth of concern of local business folks as to the future of the Cumbres & Toltec. Many of the speakers blamed the commission for the problems. These kinds of comments showed, in the eyes of one speaker, a complete lack of knowledge about the workings of that commission. "Come to the meetings," spoke Chama resident and businessperson Monica MacDowell, "and see for yourself." One person answered in the negative, pleading commitment to their small business. In the days and weeks to come, there were voices of doom and gloom. These voices were soon surpassed by the voices claiming that "the trains will run!"

Within short order, those voices of optimism were being heard in the press, on web pages and in the halls of both legislatures. David

Cargo, governor of New Mexico when the states bought the railroad, was quoted in local newspapers as urging the current governor, Gary Johnson, to do something. "That railroad is a real asset," Cargo said, "the railroad must be saved." One of the leading newspapers in New Mexico, the *Albuquerque Journal*, jumped in with an editorial October 20, urging both legislatures and Governor Johnson to take action. The editorial suggested that "[n]arrow-gauge trains are an anachronism. Their value is historic and they survive…because a few people love them and the times they represent and believe they should be preserved." Chama businesspeople knew that their survival depended on folks riding the trains during the summer.

One question kept coming up: "How are we going to get the winter shop work taken care of?" It was only too obvious to the most casual observer that the locomotives needed extensive work during the winter months. The commission had no money for it, as Bartholomew was behind in his payments to that body. Something had to be done immediately or the Cumbres & Toltec Scenic Railroad appeared doomed again.

The commission promptly put out a Request for Proposals (RFP), with the help of Stone Consulting & Design, a Pennsylvania corporation. A new operator was expected to bid on a ten-year lease, with a five-year renewal option. The commission also required a $100,000 performance bond, proof of financial resources of at least $300,000 and a bid bond of $5,000 if a company was awarded a contract but backed out later. The RFP package was an estimated three-hundred- to four-hundred-page document, which did seem a bit long to some. There was a deadline of December 10 for prospective operators to respond.

The Friends also began to act. An early November proposal was for the Friends to purchase one set of superheater tubes for one locomotive. This idea was in light of the required four- to five-month lead time, as the tubes were manufactured in Germany. At one point, this purchase was considered as a loan to the commission or a new operator. At that time, there was also discussion among Friends Board members about possibly funding a portion of the winter locomotive work. But there was no immediate decision. The Request for Proposals was scheduled for November 12. At the November 10 commission meeting, the Request for Proposals was discussed. Among the actions taken at that meeting was the appointment of a five-member Proposal Review Committee.

Members were commission chair Medardo Sanchez, Commissioner Wayne Quinlan (the son of Colorado representative Clarence Quinlan, who worked to save the railroad in the first place), Friends member Geof Gordon, Stone consultant Gary Landrio and Leo Schmitz. Naming Gordon to that committee was due, in part, to President Shaw's letter to Schmitz requesting a Friends member's role in the selection process.

This committee planned to meet in Albuquerque on December 11, with a recommendation for the entire commission at a regular meeting on the twelfth. The final decision was scheduled for December 18. Hopefully, a final decision *could* be made at that time. If all went well, a contract could be concluded, with the caveat that such an agreement had to be approved by the New Mexico State Finance Committee. That body would next meet on January 11, meaning that a new operator would not be in possession until January 17, 2000.

On November 20, 1999, the commission held an open house on the railroad for potential bidders. Dan Ranger, completing his contract with the commission, and Friends members attended the event. President Shaw and several Friends board members were in attendance. There were five interested parties in town for an extended tour of the railroad from Chama to Antonito. Those present represented both operating railroads and proposed operators. The White Pass & Yukon sent two representatives, including former chief mechanical officer John Bush. Also there were Chippewa Northwestern of Lincoln, Nebraska; Lake Erie & Ohio; Rail Ventures of Colorado; and Santa Fe Land & Cattle of New Mexico. The latter two were not known rail operators, and the Nebraska Company operated a miniature park railroad.

In conversations that evening, at least the White Pass people were most reluctant to even consider applying. They did not see any profit in running the railroad under the stipulations of the commission's request. It was also noted during the inspection that the previous operator removed all records from the property, including the Federal Railroad Locomotive Inspection reports, employee timecards and the computers from each depot. The commission did have enough money to employ the shop crew to prepare the locomotives for the annual federal inspection. This would be completed by November 23, but that was the end of its available funds. Clearly, things were a mess.

CHAPTER 11

"C&TS WILL RUN!"

The March 2000 issue of the *New Mexico Railroader* screamed this headline. A lot had happened from the dismal, bleak days of late November on through the winter. By late November, the Friends had begun to act on behalf of a now beleaguered commission and the railroad. Some voices were being heard advocating the suspension of service through 2000 in order "to put things right" on roadbed, some locomotives and rolling stock. To some, no season was better than a crippled season.

Friends treasurer Dick Cowles estimated that the lack of maintenance over the period 1997 through 1999 left the railroad with a $800,000 deficit, meaning that this figure was the amount that should have been spent on right-of-way and locomotive maintenance over the 1997–99 period. Any new operator must be prepared, it seemed, to spend that amount just to bring the railroad up to the 1996 operational level. The normal wear and tear on the locomotives during the regular season and FRA locomotive maintenance required about two major locomotive maintenance projects per year. These projects included running gear rebuild and boiler retubing by the operator each year. Projects were usually done in the off-season, in addition to other needed maintenance for reciprocating parts, appliances and tenders.

Kyle Railways did nearly two major maintenance projects each year during its tenure, including restoring Rotary OY to operating condition. Bartholomew's corporation completed only one major maintenance project in three years when six such projects were required to conform to established maintenance standards and good practice. Kyle, it must be remembered, left the property with five steam locomotives in operation, a sixth awaiting flues already purchased by Kyle and the Oahu diesel (the "Pineapple") in operating condition. Kyle also kept a second, leased diesel in Antonito principally for emergencies, which was returned to the owner by Bartholomew in 1997. In order to correct these deficiencies on the five locomotives now overdue for major work, the cost was estimated at $110,000 to $120,000 each, or a total of $570,000. The Oahu diesel needed an additional $30,000 in order to put it back into operation. All of this added up to $600,000. These figures were based on cost estimates done by Walter Rosenberger, C&TSRR Corporation's own chief mechanical officer. This was to pay for partially rebuilding their running gear, as well as other needed work. As reported in the commission minutes of the October meeting, the C&TSRR Corporation did not install the almost 3,105 ties as required by the lease. This was another deficit of about $120,000.

This lack of tie replacement further endangered the Economic Development Administration's track grant of $800,000. The installing of 2,500 ties per year was considered an in-kind contribution of $100,000 to match the $100,000 from the commission for that grant. Therefore, a new operator would either install 2,500 ties or provide an alternative source for that $100,000 match—"not only is there a deficit of $120,000, but the EDA grant [was] endangered."

Finally, Cowles noted, for the last three years there was practically no maintenance done on the passenger coaches. They had a generally "shabby" appearance, with broken seats and windows, as well as needed exterior paint. An additional $32,000 was estimated by Rosenberger for needed mechanical work. An estimated total for the coaches by the Friends came to $70,000 to $100,000. In conclusion, wrote Cowles, about $800,000 was needed "just to bring the rolling stock and track back to the condition [of] 1996. Considerable funds had to be obtained from somewhere."

At the same time Cowles was writing his estimate of monies needed for the railroad to be ready for the 2000 season, President Shaw reported on the Friends group's purchase of superheater flues. The commission cancelled some upcoming projects in order to keep a six-man shop crew to prepare four locomotives for federal inspections. Now the commission was without funds.

In a two-week period, the Friends Board continued, by electronic mail, discussions of what to do. Talks with Executive Director Leo Schmitz and veteran employees Gerald Blea and Mark Yates led to a six-week program, taking care of "necessary urgent maintenance." The upshot of these discussions were donations of almost $3,000 from the Ralph Flowers Memorial Fund, as well as two members' donations of $10,000 each to the Flowers Fund, all in order to employ the shop crew through the middle of January, the assumed time of the not-yet-named operator's taking over payroll obligations at the railroad.

During the November 20 inspection tour, several members gathered to discuss appeals to both legislatures. Geof Gordon, Dick Cowles, your author and Carl Turner met in Chama for this purpose. Turner was especially valuable due to his long years as a lobbyist for the New Mexico Rural Electrification Cooperative and service as commissioner for the railroad. This was only setting a stage for appeals to the two legislatures. The initial assumption was that Cowles, Wilson and others would assist Turner in New Mexico, while Geof Gordon, Leo Schmitz, Commissioner Louis Entz and other Friends would do the same in Colorado. As a result, Cowles continued to refine his figures before any formal appeals were made to either legislature. It was still only November 24.

On November 25, a poignant message arrived in the electronic mailboxes of the members of the Friends Board. It is worthy of a full quote in these pages:

On this Thanksgiving day, I will reflect on all that I am thankful for. This past year has been a year filled with many "challenges," to say the least. It has been a year filled with frustration and stress. So what could I possibly have to be thankful for? The answer is simply: "Friends." I am referring to the Friends of the Cumbres and Toltec Scenic Railroad.

Every year I marvel at the devotion, love, and dedication these "friends" display. And each year as I meet more and more friends, my life becomes more enriched.

I've often wondered "why?" Why do people spend their vacation time and money and come to Chama to work? I've come to realize that the work the "Friends" do is a labor of love. Love of what? Love of history?

Love of trains? Love of the scenic beauty of the area? Probably all of the above, but I think it is also a love of "friendship," comradeship, fellowship, (oops, I'm supposed to be talking about trains, not ships).

We are aware of the efforts of the Friends to provide funding and supplies to the C&TS RR so that a 6 man crew can continue work until a new operator is in place. For the new Operator, it means not having to start at "Square One." For the Friends, it is building a bridge (or trestle), over troubled water. But for us—the families of the winter shop crew—it means being able to have a Christmas this year. When things were looking pretty bleak for us, the Friends stepped in and provided the light at the end of the tunnel.

Truthfully, this year has been very hard for us, but we got through the season because we had the love and support of our Friends. Speaking for my family, we are very appreciative of your efforts. And today, when we sit down for our Thanksgiving meal, we will give thanks for all that we have been blessed with. Thank you, and Happy Thanksgiving.

Debbie S. Blea
For the Gerald M. Blea family in Chama.

With Carl Turner taking the lead, events began to move rapidly in the New Mexico legislature. Dick Cowles reported that as a result of discussions with Turner, select and key legislators were targeted for a letter writing campaign. It was true that interested parties other than the Friends were also active in promoting awareness of the needs of the railroad. C&TS engineer Jeff Stebbins was especially active in pushing a public and political agenda. But Turner's inside knowledge of the political process was vital in forming a positive and effective lobbying effort. Among those selected by Turner were Governor Johnson, State Representatives Debbie Rodella, Ben Lujan and Roberto J. Gonzales and Speaker of the House Raymond G. Sanchez. Representative Rodella was among those who had sponsored the House Memorial in praise of the Friends in the House earlier that same year. On the Senate side were Roman M. Maes III, Arthur H. Rodarte and Carlos R. Cisneros. Turner also worked to put the Friends on the agenda of Senator Roman Maes's Joint Interim Committee on Economic and Rural Development and Telecommunications, meeting in early December.

"C&TS Will Run!"

That meeting was held on December 9 at 3:30 p.m. in the state capitol. Representing the railroad was Carl Turner as unpaid lobbyist, your author and Dick Cowles for the Friends, Jeffrey Stebbins for the C&TSRR, Kim Flowers for the business community of Chama and former governor David Cargo. All present delivered presentations, at times passionate, on the historic value and the economic impact of the narrow gauge on local and statewide economies. The Friends group's estimate, based on Dick Cowles figures, showed a need for a total of $800,000 ($400,000 from each state) to put the railroad back into operating condition. Cowles pointed out that the railroad was largely self-supporting, covering 97 percent of operating and capital costs out of revenues. The railroad contributed about $45 million per year in economic benefits to the local communities. Chairman Maes and other members asked pertinent questions and showed approval of the need for funds in the current crisis. There was also some discussion of a similar presence before the Colorado legislature that the Friends, in particular, acknowledged was "in the works." The committee voted to recommend approval of the New Mexico share of $400,000.

A snowplow train clears off the C&TSRR line. This Rotary OY plow is the only rotary snowplow of its kind used in railroad clearance in the United States. This image is from the late 1970s.

At the same time, the Friends group announced funding for continuing the winter shop work in Chama. The Friends provided funding for the purchase of critical supplies and to employ the shop crew to work on locomotives for the 2000 season. President Shaw reported that $25,000 came from Friends members and other "fans of the narrow gauge" who were following the story on the Internet. She also reported that an additional $10,000 for the shop work came from the Los Alamos National Laboratory Foundation community outreach grant. In her press release, Shaw noted the role of the Friends "is to preserve the railroad and to support the Commission." The commission was now out of funds for the shop work, and "we [Friends] have some resources that can help. This critical time requires us to go beyond our usual realm of activity." By stepping in at this stage of events, the Friends can "minimize the damage that could be done to the railroad…and make it possible for the new operator to work effectively from the beginning."

The commission, in the meantime, continued to search for an operator. At the December 12 meeting in Albuquerque, Stone Consulting reported for the commission that of several proposals submitted, all "were significantly non-compliant." As a result, the search continued with a new, or amended, request released during the week of December 20. The new due date for submissions was now January 12, 2000. The original date of December 18 for a final selection of an operator was promptly cancelled.

Additional aid came on December 14 with the announcement that the New Mexico Board of Finance would loan $90,000 to the commission for emergency work on the locomotives, passenger cars and "related needs." This loan was to be paid back by April 1, 2000, but by March the "loan" had been excused. Furthermore, the political scene in New Mexico was optimistic. Governor Johnson promised support and planned to urge Governor Owens of Colorado to also join in support. Colorado commissioner Louis Entz was leading the effort in that state's legislature. Cowles called for the Friends group in Colorado to mobilize rapidly and effectively to lobby its legislators for a $400,000 request.

Efforts on the part of the Friends continued apace. On December 19, Terri Shaw notified the Friends Board of another "hole" left with Bartholomew's departure. This time it was advertising. The previous Friday, Shaw talked with Kristen Warner of the New Mexico Department of Tourism. That department published three items: *New Mexico Magazine*,

New Mexico Travel Guide (national) and *New Mexico International Travel Guide*. The C&TS had been advertised in the international guide for many years, but as the guide was published every other year, and "this is the year," it was waiting for a decision from the Friends. The advertising deadline had passed, but it was very aware of the problems involved in finding a new operator. With the commission short of funds, and the $90,000 loan not able to cover this kind of expense, Shaw said to the board, "That leaves *us* to make it happen." For an expenditure of little over $3,000, a half-page ad would be published. All of this was predicated at the time on being paid back by the new operator.

In this same message, Shaw recapped the money situation to date. In October, Treasurer Cowles reported $60,000 "available" over and above estimated year-end liabilities and monies earmarked for the Chama car repair facility and the Antonito shelter. At the last board meeting, the Friends Board voted to spend $20,000 on materials. To date, the Friends had committed about $5,800 for the flues. The $90,000 state loan was committed to wages and materials. With respect to wages, the Friends

Here's another view of the snow clearing that's necessary to operate the trains. The location is east of Chama.

delivered $20,000 to the commission—a private donation and the Los Alamos Lab grant at $10,000 each. The Ralph Flowers Fund stood at $48,208, which included three $10,000 donations. A final $25,000 was spent to cosponsor a Public Service Broadcast film with the Chama Chamber of Commerce that had been contracted for by Bartholomew but not paid for.

On December 23, Treasurer Cowles, the one person with the firmest grasp on the politics of finding the funds through both state legislatures, noted how critical time was to coordinate the Friends' lobbying efforts in both states. He recommended that "several of the Friends involved in lobbying in each state ought to meet with Leo and some of the Commissioners in Antonito to try to achieve a united front." That meeting was held in Antonito with representatives from the commission and the Friends. Present were Leo and Maria Schmitz, Wayne Quinlan, Louis Entz, Bob Akers, Jerry Sahnd, your author and Dick Cowles. The consensus reached was for the commission to request a total of $460,000 for Colorado and $410,000 from New Mexico for the 2001 fiscal year. The Friends group was to mobilize support in each state for this effort.

At that same meeting, Leo Schmitz reported on current work by the shop crew. About $18,000 of the Friends and Los Alamos funds went toward wages through December 16. Cowles said that there was still about $12,000 available for that purpose, without using the $90,000 New Mexico loan. After that, there were still Friends funds available "on a loan basis" for "critical materials." There was the decision made to coordinate the approach to each governor, with Louis Entz in Colorado and Carl Turner in New Mexico. Cowles concluded, "I should emphasize that today's meeting was timely, truly constructive, and noteworthy for the spirit of cooperation throughout." The whole project was entering a very critical phase: the political arena.

Later, on January 13, while everyone waited for answers to the newest Request for Proposals, President Shaw wrote to Schmitz a summary of funds raised by the Friends. The Flowers Fund stood at $42,000 from donations, and a check for that amount was on the way to Schmitz. The Friends group had previously sent to the commission $20,000 earmarked for shop crew wages, utilities and materials. Within the $42,000 were amounts specified by the donors: $2,500 for crew wages and another $2,000 for "a load of coal and a new fax machine for the Chama depot." Shaw further wrote:

It is our wish that the balance be used according to the following priorities:

For parts such as air pumps and gaskets and materials such as brass for bushings, wedges, etc., tires, and other running gear components.

For materials and labor which cannot be performed in Chama, such as the recontouring of drivers at the Durango shops or work on air pumps.

For gas, electricity and welding supplies for the shop.

Wages for shop labor, but only after further discussion with me.

Shaw also discussed administration, monthly reports, copies of invoices and the like. Money was still coming in through donations, and this would be sent on to the commission periodically. The Friends group was withholding an amount in the Flowers Fund to use as a match to the Los Alamos National Laboratory Foundation for a grant of $10,000 for asbestos removal from locomotives #492 and #483. The letter ended with perhaps the understatement of the season: "We are pleased to be able to provide this help to restore the railroad to operation."

Amid all of the worries and speculation of the day, there was also another change. Colorado governor Owens made a sudden change on the Colorado commission. Longtime member Wayne Quinlan of Antonito, whose father was one of the principals in the early move to purchase the railroad, was replaced by Friends member Carol Salisbury. Mrs. Salisbury is employed as field representative for U.S. senator Wayne Allard of Colorado. Louis Entz remained as the other commissioner from Colorado.

Finally, there were results from the commission request sent to the Selection Committee. The *Albuquerque Journal North* on January 20 reported that there were three remaining bidders. Chippewa Northwestern of Lincoln, Nebraska, "[o]perates a small steam-powered railroad [fifteen-inch gauge] on the grounds of the Seward County Historical Society Museum, about 25 miles west of Lincoln." Also bidding was Rail Ventures of Louisville, Colorado, an organization that "has no known track record since it has never operated a railroad." Then there was San Juan Mountain Railroad of Albuquerque, but the paper reported that "[i]nformation on San Juan wasn't available Wednesday." The state Public Regulation Commission doesn't list the company as being a registered corporation in New Mexico.

The paper also reported that "two other previous bidders, Alaska-based White Pass & Yukon and Albuquerque-based Old Santa Fe Land and Cattle Ltd., dropped out of the bidding and didn't submit new bids."* The Selection Committee spent thirteen hours that Friday. Each proposal was scored. The committee recommended further talks be held with Rail Ventures and San Juan Mountain Railroad. Discussion would continue. With this rather discouraging prospect, there were renewed suggestions from outside the commission and the Friends for canceling the 2000 season in order to rebuild.

On January 22, Medardo Sanchez Jr., chairman of the commission, again thanked the Friends "for their continuous efforts, time and finances to keep the Locomotive project functioning." As if listening to the voices of doom, Sanchez went on to say that those "endeavors have made running the C&TS RR for the 2000 Season more of a reality." The coming season was the railroad's thirtieth anniversary, and a celebration was in order.

Events began to move rapidly for the Friends, the commission and the railroad. At a Finance Committee meeting on Saturday, January 22, among other business matters, President Shaw announced a major change in her life, as well for the future of the Friends. "The greatest source of stress in my life right now is from the tug of war that I experience every day between doing Friends' work and my law work. It is aggravated by the fact that the Friends work is interesting and dynamic and the law work is not." Shaw went on to explain that along with the expanding role of the Friends' activities and "events currently transpiring at the railroad the great opportunity that [these activities] present for the Friends, what I truly would prefer to do is Friends' work." Howard and Terri felt the "tug" of the narrow-gauge country and concluded that they would move to New Mexico. Moreover, Shaw would propose that "I become the Executive Director for the Friends." The hiring of an executive director had been the subject of some considerable discussion for some time. In 1999, a consultant gave his opinion that, as a mature and proven not-for-profit organization, it was time for such a move. The matter of a executive director was scheduled for the next board meeting. For this and other important matters, Shaw called for a special board meeting on February 12 in Albuquerque.

As for the selection of an operator, Shaw also reported on the commission activities as she heard from Geof Gordon, Friends

This is the C&TSRR Rotary Snowplow OM, powered by two engines, cleaning the tracks in the "narrows," just east of Chama, New Mexico.

representative to the Selection Committee. That committee met on the previous Friday for thirteen hours. There were three bidders with, as Geof noted, no significant steam railroad tourist experience. All of the bids had deficiencies, and none of the bids was very appealing. The committee recommended rejecting one and continuing discussions with the other two.

The letters were sent, with noon on Wednesday, January 26, as a deadline. The interviews were scheduled for Friday, January 28, and then the committee would meet and make its recommendation. The commission planned a meeting for January 29 in Alamosa.

Shaw noted some inferences in the committee statement, leading to the possibility that these remaining bids might be rejected. Geof indicated some "inclination" for that to happen, but that was up to the commission. Discussion between Shaw and one commissioner seemed to lead in that direction. The final two bidders were not "adequate."

Gordon explained that if the commission did reject these remaining bids, the legal process required for the Request for Proposals would be satisfied and the process would be over. Then, as Geof put it, it is "open season." This meant that the commission was free to talk with any "potential" operator and enter into any suitable agreement.

The Selection Committee and Gary Landrio of Stone Consulting reported that there was discussion of a nonprofit operation. Should such an operator be considered? Landrio referred to his company's experience with other similar tourist operations. He said that such an option was indeed "viable and not bizarre." He did caution that such an arrangement worked only when the nonprofit corporation was managed in the same manner as a for-profit corporation.

This report by Gordon led Shaw to hold informal talks with the assembled members of the Development Committee on Sunday, January 22 and 23, in Claremont, California. This was called as a meeting of the Finance Committee, but it was indeed a true representation of thoughtful folks. There was a consensus in that group, as well as similar agreement arising from informal talks held the previous August as the crisis on the railroad developed, that the Friends Board could support an effort to operate the railroad. The idea developed at that time was to form a subsidiary corporation to actually manage the operation of the railroad. There were legal and tax matters to be addressed, as well as consider how much capital was necessary.

Dick Cowles had assembled and analyzed financial records from both the Kyle and Bartholomew records in the course of the lobbying effort. As a result, he estimated that capital needs were about $350,000. There was other evidence that a cash balance of $350,000 and a credit line of $125,000 were required.

The source of such capital was discussed, whether to be through repayable loans and/or donations. Just that weekend, after a few phone calls, a total of $100,000 was pledged, with an additional $150,000 also pledged from one donor. The latter donor resulted from a press release sent out in November. Further calls brought in another $40,000, with yet two more unspecified amounts. These amounts were also adequate collateral for a credit line at the bank.

Raising money was easier, however, than matters of finding management. An appeal to former manager Joe Vigil of Chama brought forth an offer as "unpaid consultant" but not a return as full-time manager. A general manager, office manager and chief mechanical officer were very open positions at this point.

166

The underlining reasons for the lack of bids by experienced steam tourist line operators lay, Shaw found, in the present requirements asked for by the commission. The commission placed all of the responsibility of maintaining track, rolling stock and rent on the operator. This left the operator with very little or no profit. This meant that the commercial operators such as Durango & Silverton, Georgetown Loop, White Pass & Yukon and Wheeling & Lake Erie did not bother to answer the second Request. Georgetown Loop and the White Pass apparently did offer to hold further talks about operating but on vastly different terms. Essentially, they wanted an agreement to be merely a management team for the commission and not as the operator, taking full responsibility for the line.

On the political front, there were indications of growing support in both legislatures for the appropriations requested by the commission. Comment seemed to show more support now than at any time in the past. The only problem for the commission seemed to be the inability to find an operator. Therefore, Dick Cowles and Carl Turner were to attend a Finance Committee meeting in Santa Fe on January 27, 2000.

The result of that committee hearing was a small but positive step, as reported by Dick Cowles. The committee, in a usual manner, agreed unanimously to table the funding request. That meant that the request was placed on a growing pile of similar spending requests. These were sent on to subsequent hearings by other committees. Those later hearings make the real decisions as to the fate of such requests—to approve, drop or make drastic cuts.

The commission planned another meeting on January 29 in the lengthening search for an operator. Two days earlier, on Thursday, January 27, Dick Cowles reported to Leo Schmitz on the results of the New Mexico appropriations committee meeting. During that conversation, Schmitz asked Cowles who from the Friends group would attend the upcoming commission meeting. Schmitz said that he would like someone from the Friends to make a public statement concerning whatever ideas the Friends group was developing for operation of the railroad. Cowles reported this event to Terri Shaw. She and Cowles then reported to the new commissioner Carol Salisbury and the commissioner Medardo Sanchez. Shaw also brought Salisbury up to date on what the Friends had done so far. Her reaction was gratitude for the information and the expression that these Friends' actions, past, present and future, appeared to be a way out of the dilemma for the commission and a new operator. Cowles reported that Medardo Sanchez's reaction was that it "made his day."

As a result, Terri Shaw, Dick Cowles, Geof Gordon and John West developed a statement asking the commission for three weeks to develop a formal proposal. Leo Schmitz responded with, "Can't you act sooner?" There were still two bids for the commission to survey plus an offer from Lindsey Ashby of Georgetown Loop Railroad, offering management assistance to the commission for a fee to operate the railroad for the next year or two. In that interval, the commission might have time to find a permanent solution to the operation problem.

In both situations, either the Friends proposal or Ashby's offer depended on the commission's actions at the January 29 meeting regarding the two remaining proposals. Just minutes before that meeting, Leo Schmitz was advised by Colorado attorney general Rod Wolthoff to be very cautious in the public statement. Wolthoff said that Dick Cowles should only express the Friends' willingness and desire to help the commission in any way. So, Cowles amended his statement to something "emotional" about this being the thirtieth year of the railroad, how important "it" was to all of us and the region and that the Friends group stood willing to help the commission in any way it could. Things were coming to a head.

CHAPTER 12

"C&TS WILL RUN!" PART II

The January 29 meeting in Alamosa was pivotal to the future of the railroad. There were still two applicants to operate the railroad, San Juan Mountain Railroad Company and Rail Ventures. The commission dealt with a few ceremonial matters before turning to the main business of finding an operator.

Colorado assistant attorney general Rod Wolthoff reported that the Evaluation Committee and the full commissioners met with San Juan Mountain and Rail Ventures. They concluded that neither company was adequate for the job of running the railroad. The commission accepted the report. Chairman Medardo then asked Wolthoff as to the next step. Wolthoff replied that the commission had three options: amend the official Request and ask for new proposals, seek a potential contractor to operate the railroad and to enter into contract discussions or operate the railroad itself. Left with these options, the chairman set a meeting for the following Wednesday, February 2, at 3:00 p.m. in the Antonito Town Hall boardroom.

Chairman Sanchez asked Dick Cowles for a report on the capital appropriation meeting of January 28. Dick reported that Representative Debbie Rodella submitted a bill for the full $400,000. Commissioner Lewis Entz said that a similar amount was progressing well in Colorado.

After an Executive Session, the commission returned to instruct Leo Schmitz to explore different options and to report at the next meeting. The options were that the commission run the railroad, look for another potential and successful operator or "see if any other viable options exist." The meeting adjourned.

Over the next few days, until the next commission meeting, there were messages and phone calls from many interested Friends and others. There were still serious reservations voiced among some former volunteers and members of earlier rescue groups about the Friends trying to make a proposal. There were more conversations with potential operators, with most replying in the negative for various reasons—track work, insurance or letters of interest but not a bid. The Georgetown folks continued to offer a management team for a limited time. There were also voices raised in support of the Friends, especially as a nonprofit organization with a proven record in fundraising and historic preservation work. Some worried that there might be some lack of objectivity in playing the role of operator while continuing the work of historic preservation.

Meantime, the Friends group's lobbying effort in the legislature continued to bear fruit. On February 1, the New Mexico House Transportation Committee voted in favor of the railroad money. Presenting the case before the committee was Representative Rodella, Medardo Sanchez, Carl Turner, Leo Schmitz and Dick Cowles.

Another tidbit of good news arrived from the Friends office in Albuquerque. An update of renewals of memberships as of February 2 showed remarkable increases. The total renewing were 1,015, with total contributions of $74,208.99. This amounted to an average contribution of $73.11. This was an impressive figure in light of the basic family membership of $25.00! The number renewing above that basic level was 592, and the percentage above the basic amount was 58 percent. In 1999, membership did not go above 1,000 renewals until March. In comparison with last year, with 71 percent of the returns, the Friends have contributions amounting to 98 percent of last year's contributions. This was a remarkable show of concern and confidence by the membership over the genuine fears for the future of the railroad.

Chairman Sanchez called the February 2 meeting to order at 3:15 p.m. with a room full of interested folks. Following the approval of the January 29 minutes, the commission turned to the pressing matter of a new operator. Consultant Gary Landrio reported being in touch with the Wheeling & Lake Erie, Gulf & Ohio and the Ohio Central Railroads, all previous bidders in 1996. Each of them said that it was not interested in submitting a proposal.

He also reported no responses from the Manitou & Pikes Peak Railway. Landrio did talk with John Bush of the White Pass & Yukon and noted that it was interested but had several "reservations and conditions." Schmitz reported that he had been in touch with the Friends group and that it was interested and was putting together information and preparing a proposal.

As a result, Commissioner Entz moved to terminate the Request for Proposals (or not issue a new one). The motion passed. Chairman Sanchez then directed Entz, Dr. Lynn and Leo Schmitz to meet with representatives of the Friends to discuss a proposal by the Friends. He also asked Landrio and Schmitz to continue talks with White Pass & Yukon. Before adjournment, Sanchez set the next meeting for February 16 in Chama. The commission also agreed to hire someone to man the telephones in Chama to take any reservations that might come in.

The Friends responded to the invitation at that meeting that it was "indeed" interested but that it would take action agreeable to the board. The Friends Board planned to meet on February 12. The commission and Colorado attorney general were most anxious for faster action—a day or two! The four Friends present—Geof Gordon, Steve Schroeder, Dick Cowles and your author—hurriedly met. We agreed to try to have two or three directors meet with Commissioners Entz and Lynn and Executive Director Schmitz in a day or two in Chama. This delay permitted a chance for the Executive Committee to have a phone conference "to provide guidance."

The commissioners were now anxious to conclude an arrangement with the Friends, since there was no real movement with any of the other potential operators. Gary Landrio, by phone, and some of the commissioners were "quite candid" in noting the lack of results. There were operators that did not answer or that raised conditions about track work and insurance, for example, that were too big for them to consider operating under the conditions of the Request.

Cowles continued his report to the directors by saying, "It's clear that the Commission would prefer to do business with [Friends]. But [the Friends group was] going to have to take a very careful look at the…risks and potential liabilities, no matter what the potential positives for the Friends, for the railroad, and for the communities."

This decision by the commission to turn to the Friends did not meet with universal agreement. Both Rail Ventures and San Juan Mountain

Railroad were reported in the *Journal North* the next day as threatening protests. In fact, both did later write letters of protest, but both attorneys general were on record that the process went to the end and was closed. The time for the Friends drew closer.

On February 6, Cowles reported that New Mexico House Appropriations and Finance Committee continued to support the request for funds. Similar support appeared in the Senate, and similar requests were moving in Colorado. There were still some negative comments on the Internet by those who were sure that the railroad would not run in 2000. On the other hand, on February 7, the first "Locomotive Work Expense & Billing—Report #1" arrived from Executive Director Schmitz to President Shaw. A spreadsheet accompanied Schmitz's letter showing expenditures to date of $32,154.77 of the original $62,000.00. The remaining $29,845.23 was marked for continued locomotive work. He also expressed the gratitude of the commission.

Discussions among the Friends officers and board of directors started immediately after the February 2 meeting and before the February 12 meeting of the Friends Board. The Executive Committee met by phone for two hours on February 3 to prepare for the planned negotiating session, with the commission slated for February 6. In that process, there were several key issues, such as working capital, liability insurance, the EDA track grant, the term and escape clause, state appropriations, fares, payments to the commission, the performance bond, staffing, inventory and the season start and ride structure. The February 16 meeting of Entz, Schmitz, Gordon and Cowles discussed these issues in preparation for both the commission meeting and the Friends Board meeting. "In all, a very promising start," reported Cowles. (A confidential memorandum regarding the Friends group's potential offer was sent to the commission on February 15 in anticipation of the meeting on the sixteenth.)

Cowles prepared a financial "model" of possible cash flows during an operating period of more than fifteen months from March 2000 to May 2001. In his opinion, this was the most critical period. All of this was for the discussions on February 12. His general conclusion was under "Sources of Funds…necessary to offset the red ink—$400,000 of state money [each] for the locomotives and a similar amount of working capital…that is our price of admission." On the ninth, Cowles wrote to Mr. William Valdes, House Appropriations and Finance Committee chief of staff, outlining the necessary funds disposition. He pointed out the Friends' donations to date and asked for a minimum of $200,000 for locomotive restoration and another $50,000 to help save the EDA track grant. These amounts were to be matched in equal sums by the Colorado legislature. He also asked for support for the commission to pay back the $90,000 "loan" from New Mexico Board of Finance (later "excused") and another $67,000 for legal expenses in terminating the former operator's contract and legal expenses. There were several other bills introduced in support of the railroad, but "it does appear that Bill 203 is the one most on point."

Finally, the day of decision for the Friends arrived. That was the special board meeting on February 12, 2000, in Albuquerque. After several reports and other actions, including naming Warren Smalley to fill a board vacancy, the board took up Item 5 on the agenda: the "Proposal to the RR Commission to Operate the Railroad." At that meeting, the board approved the following resolution:

> The Board of Directors of the Friends of the Cumbres & Toltec Scenic Railroad, a New Mexico 503c3 Corporation, resolves to: (1) endorse presenting a proposal to the Cumbres & Toltec Railroad Commission for the formation of a new not-for-profit corporation to operate the Cumbres & Toltec Scenic Railroad; (2) sponsor the new corporation; and (3) create a steering committee to work on details of the proposal and thereafter form the corporation if approved by the Commission.

No sooner had the Friends Board of Directors acted to bid on operations than it was a matter of just how this was to be done. At that same board meeting, President Shaw outlined a plan to create a second operating company completely divorced from the Friends itself. The idea behind this move came from the question of personal liability. The fear that should a serious accident occur, the members of the Friends Board, as well as the operating board and the general membership, would be held accountable. One member noted that as things stood on February 16, the Friends group seemed to have no connection with the new company at all. "As it stands now we cannot say, 'The Friends operates the railroad.'" The railroad would be operated by a totally separate entity with no connection to the Friends Board. "The Commission," the member wrote, "expects the Friends to propose how they would operate the railroad, not some unaffiliated party…I think that we, the Board of the Friends, have a responsibility to the railroad, the communities and our membership to have direct oversight of the operating company." There were other voices raised with the same concerns. They all generally agreed on the need for oversight or control, and all urged seeking legal expertise regarding nonprofit corporations.

The Sunday morning, February 13 *Albuquerque Journal* said it all: "Fans Vote to Take Over Rail Operations." President Shaw also appointed a subsidiary board to manage operations: Warren Smalley, president; Geof Gordon, vice-president; Dick Cowles, treasurer; John West, secretary; and Joe Vigil. By facsimile and letter, the Friends advised the commission of its decision and that the letter would constitute the proposal.

This six-page letter started by addressing the key issues in preparing the railroad for operation starting in May and thence to operate for the 2000 season. Excerpts follow, highlighting the main points:

> **Financial Commitments.** *The Friends deposited over $300,000 in a Chama bank which "is immediately available."" The sum was in addition to the $60,000 already transmitted for locomotive repairs. The Friends now have at least $300,000 in "working capital." That fund "will exceed" the above amount and the Friends will add more money as needed.*

> **Corporate structure.** *As of this date, the Friends were creating (two weeks hence) a new five member Board of Directors for the new corporation, which will operate the railroad. Their resumes were included with this proposal. Their individual skills include a former general manager of the railroad, a career railroad industry executive, and others with business management experience and "long-standing interest in railroading." The new corporation is the present Rio Grande Railroad Preservation Corporation [RGRPC].*
>
> *The new corporation was a not-for-profit entity and will not pay dividends "of any type." "All net proceeds from receipts will go toward the labor and materials required to restore and improve the equipment, track, and structures of the Railroad, all of which will contribute to the benefit of the region and its people."*

Management. *"The* [RGRPC] *Board of Directors, together with the General Manager, would act as a management committee for the railroad. Members of the board would be immediately and intimately involved in marketing and financial matters and would operate the Chama office until a General Manager is in place." That would happen as soon as possible but was not critical at the moment. Winter shop work was already proceeding.*

The General Manager will be in charge of daily operations. The General Manager will hire operating staff with as many as possible being selected from Chama and Antonito areas, unless "suitably qualified candidates cannot be found."

Management in daily operations was not to differ significantly from that of the previous operators. The Board anticipated hiring from the employee pool utilized by the previous operators. The Corporation did reserve "the right to organize itself in the most effective manner and to change that [management] *structure as needs require."*

Operations. *The plan is to open the railroad on Memorial Day weekend 2000. Regular service will be from both terminals. The RGRPC Corporation did reserve the right to make schedule changes depending on conditions.*

Improvements to Equipment and Infrastructure. *Track and equipment has suffered from deferred maintenance for three years. "The Friends has already granted $60,000 to the Commission for major repairs to locomotives that started last November and is continuing." Friends also played "a key role in lobbying for over $800,000 in funding from the States of Colorado and New Mexico, including matching funds to ensure the availability of the U.S. Economic Development Administration grant for track work." The new money is to be used for immediate track repairs and overhaul of locomotives and coaches.*

The RGRPC would hire a general manager and mechanical and track supervisory personnel, with the proper leadership and technical skills, to ensure that these programs are pushed. In addition to that work done by regular employees, contractors will be needed to catch up on the backlog of deferred maintenance.

Locomotive work was being done. Track work will depend on the weather and ground frost. Coachwork may be augmented by volunteer labor with railroad supervision to prepare for opening day.

Marketing and Sales. *"As soon as possible the Corporation will engage an experienced advertising agency…There* [are] *already contracts for advertising in major regional travel journals and in select rail-related publications…There will be a sales and reservation office established with a reservation system. Sales brochures are ordered and that we anticipate quickly hiring an experienced marketer."*

Financial Projections. *Enclosed were cash flow projections for the first 15-month period starting March 1, 2000. This was the period "which we believe the railroad faces its greatest financial risks." "As indicated, based upon the Corporation providing $400,000 in initial working capital, and the receipt of $400,000 for locomotive rehabilitation from the states between this June and May 2001, the working capital balance is projected to reach a low of $5,000 by the end of May 2000, just before start-up of the revenue season. This is due to the significant and necessary expenditures that we expect to incur between March and May to prepare the railroad for operations—a period without compensating revenues."*

"Assuming a ridership of 45,000 (later raised to 50,000) paying passengers in 2000, by the season's end in October our analysis projects that cumulative cash flow should swing sharply to the positive in line with past trends. The bulk of these gains would then be allocated to continuing our aggressive shop program for restoration of locomotives and other equipment through the winter of 2000–2001. As a consequence, we expect the cash balance to again decline sharply to a $90,000 level before the start of the 2001-revenue season, this being a level we feel prudent. Please note that these projections do not include EDA grant monies, since we are assuming that cash received will equal cash spent on this vital work."

"This proposal is made subject to our negotiation of a mutually satisfactory lease based on the proposed document provided to us by the Commission. We are prepared to begin those negotiations immediately."

Signed by Richard J. Cowles, Member of the Board and Treasurer, Friends of the Cumbres & Toltec Scenic Railroad. February 15, 2000. Enclosures include Biographies of Board Members and Cash Flow Analysis.

Of course, nothing could happen until the commission acted, and that action came at the February 16 meeting in Chama. The commission did have one other offer from a potential operator on the table aside from that of the Friends. The White Pass & Yukon submitted a second offer to provide a management team with the commission to supply the funds needed for track and rolling stock work. At the meeting, the commission rejected that offer since there was no money for that kind of arrangement. Furthermore, the management fee for White Pass's services was higher than any income the commission received from previous operators.

The commissioners then turned to the Friends group's proposal. The members established that the promised $300,000 cash was deposited in the Friends' Chama bank account. They noted that the Friends had donated $62,000 for the winter shop program. They also noted that the Friends contributed the necessary money for a movie contract, for a film planned by Public Broadcasting to be shown throughout the country later that year, as well as that the Friends paid to advertise the railroad to keep the C&TS before the traveling public in the summer season. The commission noted that the Friends' strong management team was in place and that the team was further strengthened by the addition of Mr. Joe Vigil of Chama. As a former manager, his inclusion on the team was a major asset. Finally, they added that more discussions were needed in the areas of marketing and maintenance.

The commission then voted unanimously for Leo Schmitz and two commissioners to negotiate with the Friends group to operate the railroad. Dick Cowles and Geof Gordon were to represent the Friends. Commissioner Lewis Entz noted the pressure of time and urged early negotiations in order to have a contract signed by the first week of March. There were some legal niceties, which were addressed by the commission in a press release on February 16. In that release, the commission made a very important point of avoiding any hint of conflict of interest between the commission and the Friends: "Commission members are either honorary or active volunteer members of the Friends" but "do not serve on the board of directors of the Friends or participate in their decisions." Commissioners are not involved "in formation of the new non-profit corporation or [any] decision to submit a proposal on behalf of this new corporation." The commissions had no investment in nor were they members of the new corporation.

Based on a confidential memorandum dated February 16, 2000, the Friends group sent a proposal to the commission based on the discussions between the two parties on February 6. The commissioners had requested a meeting between themselves and representatives of the Friends before the Friends Board meeting on the twelfth, "at which time the Friends would decide whether to go forward with a proposal to operate the railroad." The February 16 memorandum was a summary of "these discussions and our understandings." There were several "threshold issues" that required agreement before the Friends could proceed with a proposal to operate the railroad.

Liability insurance was always an expensive matter to all previous operators. Kyle handled the matter by simply including the C&TS into already existing policy for its other railroads. Both Scenic and Bartholomew found this to be a very expensive item. The Friends, therefore, put the matter of liability insurance in the hands of the commission. As landlord, the Friends group said, this was a commission responsibility, with RGRPC paying the premiums, up to about $70,000 per annum, and the RGRPC be a "named insured." The Economic Development Administration's track work grant had to be altered to allow work to be done in various critical places on the right-of-way in the mountains. The original grant specified the first twelve miles out of Antonito. This was another "threshold issue" for the Friends.

A term and escape clause provided for a five-year initial term, renewable for two successive five-year terms. Also, either party should be able to terminate the lease in any year with a ninety-day notice, effective on October 31.

All parties agreed that to continue operations of the railroad beyond the 2000 season could not happen unless the states appropriated a total of $400,000 for locomotive work and $100,000 for the track work grant. "In the event of a shortfall the Friends would have to give notice by August 1, 2000, to cancel its lease." There was general agreement that the ticket prices for the 2000 season should be close to those for 1999.

In the past, the commission earned money from the operation based on various formulas, a percent of the base ticket sales, a different percent of food and shop concession sales and so forth. A much simpler formula was needed. Since the Friends had already made significant contributions, and there was the probability of state money for 2000, there was "common understanding…that the Friends (RGRPC) would not make any payments to the Commission in the first year for capital projects." The Friends would pay to cover the commission's operating costs not covered by state appropriations. That might amount to $70,000 to $80,000. It was commonly understood that this matter might well change in coming years. "The group agreed that a method of joint decision on the uses of excess revenues should be devised." The requirement for a performance bond was dropped, and the Friends (RGRPC) group was made responsible for staffing. Both parties agreed to an inventory before a lease could be signed.

For the first season, the Friends group offered (and the commission agreed) to start operations on Memorial weekend. There would be one train from each terminal each day, but with the proviso that for the first three weeks trains would run only on weekends. This allowed for maintenance of track and rolling stock. The Friends group also asked for the flexibility for additional rides beyond the two trains from each end. These ideas were the basis for discussions. There were other voices raised with the same concerns. They all generally agreed on the need for oversight or control and all urged seeking legal expertise regarding non-profit corporations. This question was to be addressed in the very near future.

On February 17, the commission responded to the Friends' proposal by fax asking for some more information and clarification. The commission wanted more details of the legal name and address of the operator, including incorporation details (names, dates and references). Furthermore, it needed information "concerning its financial, profession background and experience" in tourist railroads and other such experiences. Office procedures were also requested, including audited financial statements, recordkeeping and the like. A date of February 24 was set for a meeting of the commission and the Friends group in Alamosa.

President Shaw immediately called for a phone conference of the new board, Bill Lock and herself. This group was to provide answers to the commission by February 23. These materials were due just before noon on the twenty-third, as the next day was the momentous meeting. On February 24, the commission agreed that the Friends group's support company (RGRPC) would be the new operator of the Cumbres & Toltec Scenic Railroad.

On March 2, President Shaw sent a congratulatory message to all involved in putting together "our proposal and shepherded it through the process." She thanked the new board (Smalley, Gordon, Cowles and West plus John Craft) for "countless phone calls and phone conferences." She especially thanked Dick Cowles for the effort to "synthesize and summarize all the information" and for "the unenviable task of collating the team's comments…into a coherent presentation" for Assistant Attorney General Rod Woltoff of Colorado. "How lucky we are to have such a fine group of people to commit so much of their time to make this happen."

All the while, work continued on the locomotives in Chama, and the political process continued apace in Santa Fe and Denver. Support for the railroad came from all across the nation and from foreign countries. It all worked! On March 8, Governor Johnson of New Mexico signed the appropriation bill for $400,000. Governor Bill Owen of Colorado followed suit about one month later.

On the web page for the Rio Grande Railway Preservation Corporation, "an affiliate of the Friends" announced on March 15 that Edward M. McLaughlin was the new general manager of the railroad. McLaughlin came with many years of experience in railroad operations and steam locomotive experience. His more recent experience was managing a freight car repair facility and handling loading of oceangoing freight. Before that, he was CEO of the Northwestern Pacific Railroad, a three-hundred-mile line with freight and seasonal passenger services. He had been president and general manager of the Fort Worth & Western and also a freight and steam excursion railroad. In the 1970s, he had been general superintendent of the steam-powered Texas State Railroad.

Meanwhile, the Friends group and the RGRPC waited for final approval from both states for the lease agreement. Work, however, continued in Chama, with special attention paid to the locomotives. Gerald Blea reported in detail on work performed during the winter on locomotives #497, #489, #488 and #487. Plans were to have three locomotives operating by opening and maybe four or five by the end of the season. "We can and we will!" said Blea. Chama businessperson Kim Flowers was hired for advertising and public relations. By March 20, another Chama businessperson, Candie Martinez, had taken over as office manager. Passenger operations were scheduled to begin on Sunday, May 27.

On March 30, the New Mexico Board of Finance met to consider "Approval of Operator Agreement." There were representatives of both boards, Friends and RGRPC, present. After a little discussion, mostly to make sure that Colorado was in agreement, they did vote unanimously to approve! This was the final moment. Agreement by this board meant that the Friends and RGRPC were in the railroad operating business. The expectation was to take possession of the "premises" on April 1. On March 30, President Smalley wrote a progress report for the Friends Board. Recounting the hiring of the general manager, the locomotive work in progress and the hiring of professional help for the track work, along with regular C&TS crews, he outlined the work for early April. The Durango & Silverton offered to help, if needed. A temporary reservation system was in place, with more than four thousand reservations made. The public relations and office managers were hired, and plans for opening day were put in place. A special event was planned for Friday, June 16, as an open house for governors and legislators. Indeed, representatives of both boards toured the New Mexico legislative halls during a special session, thanking the legislators, giving each a book about the railroad and inviting all to June festivities. The Federal Railroad Administration planned to inspect locomotives, cars, bridges and track between May 15 and 19.

This was a welcome act, as it would seem to justify confidence in a safe, operating railroad. Even more inspiring, Smalley said, was having about $400,000 in the bank. Plans called for fifty-one thousand riders during the 2000 season in order to make it through the season without resorting to more fundraising. "Overall," Smalley wrote, "we are optimistic that we have the resources and plans in place to effectively run the railroad." In early April, the Colorado legislature appropriated the funds for the railroad. On opening day, the steam-powered trains started out from Chama and Antonito, just as they had since 1881.

SUMMARY

By the thirtieth year of state ownership of the Cumbres & Toltec Scenic Railroad, the various volunteer groups had come full circle. In the beginning, there were those dedicated folks who worked to save the railroad for posterity and economic development. After the states bought the railroad, the volunteers had to search for new roles. They were left out of actually running trains, so they finally opted for diminished roles as car attendants and in publishing activities and restoration projects. As noted in this narrative, that entire movement finally fell by the wayside in the late 1970s. So, too, did the then operator. In the decade of the 1980s, two important developments affected the survival of the C&TSRR. One was the very successful operation directed by Kyle Railways wherein new levels of operations and passenger loads greatly increased, and the line became even better known worldwide. A second development was the advent of a new volunteer organization, the Friends of the C&TSRR. This group was destined to have a profound impact on the railroad and in a manner not anticipated beyond historic preservation—the actual running of trains.

In the 1990s, however, major trouble appeared to cast a pall of doom over the now famous but endangered railroad. The third operator fell out of favor with the commission and the Friends due to his lack of maintenance of the operating structure—track, locomotives, passenger cars and so forth. A diligent search for another operator failed, and a sense of despair settled over the whole enterprise. There was, thankfully, a proven organization standing in the wings. The Friends group provided reserves of money to keep the shop operating and, therefore, keep alive hope that things might be set right while wishing for a replacement operator somewhat in the mold of Kyle Railways. Taking rather tentative steps, at first denying any interest in operating the railroad, the Friends continued to move in that direction. As no qualified candidates for the operator appeared, the early informal discussions resolved into firm action to ensure that the trains would run in 2000 and beyond by taking hold of operations if need be. The volunteers had come full circle to save the railroad a second time.

EPILOGUE

The Friends proceeded to organize a separate company, the Rio Grande Railroad Preservation Corporation, to actually handle the day-to-day operations of the railroad. This group was also beset by unforeseen and unfortunate events. The summer of the great fire at Los Alamos, New Mexico, caused the forest service to shut down the railroad for one month in the middle of the season. Also, the Federal Railroad Administration issued new rules for steam boilers that had the effect of leaving RGRPC with only one operable locomotive. Both events had the effect of reducing income to levels that caused the corporation to give up the contract to run trains. As of February 2006, the Friends group was again setting up a separate company to run trains during the 2006 season. All were optimistic that this would happen; trains did run. The 2006 season was a great success, with just over forty thousand riders. The volunteers had saved the railroad a third time. Plans for the coming seasons are in the works, and all looks to be doing very well.

Notes

Chapter 2: Material for this chapter came from interviews with Carl Turner, Eddie Vigil, Carmen and Earl Knoob and former New Mexico governor David Cargo; the October 27, 1960 *Albuquerque Journal*; the Department of Interior, Information Service, Bureau of Reclamation press release of October 27, 1960; and a contract between the United States of America and the Denver & Rio Grande Western Railroad Company for relocating segments of the company's railroad line to bypass Navajo Reservoir, October 28, 1960, and February 27, 1962. See also *The Collected Colorado Rail Annual*, issues 1–7, "They're Still Building Narrow Gauge in Colorado" (1974): 31–33. Finally, see also Eleanor Daggett's *Chama, New Mexico Recreation Center: Its History, Industries, Recreation* (Albuquerque, NM: Starline Corporation, 1973, A Nature Trek Publication).

Chapter 4: Material for this chapter came from NGRRA *Telltale* and files, commission files and minutes and the *Albuquerque Journal*.

Chapter 5: At the time, Jim Demlow was employed at the New Mexico Institute of Mining and Technology, Socorro. He and his wife, June, owned the Chama Station Inn in town. Each weekend, he commuted the 240-plus miles between Socorro and Chama. See also Ralph Hawes's "The Moonlight (Midnight) Special," *Slim Gauge News* 4, no. 3 (Fall 1974): 46–47. The author was appointed to the CPRC by Governor Bruce King. I subsequently became chairman of the Railroad Subcommittee. I was not a railroad historian. I became acquainted with the eminent historian Vernon J. Glover and began to learn. Glover became an unofficial advisor to the CPRC and to me. Regarding State Engineer Reynolds, the author was present and heard Reynolds speak of his credentials.

Material for this chapter came from NGRRA files, commission files, the *Slim Gauge News* and *La Cronica de Nuevo Mexico*, March 1979. The society was established in 1859, making it the oldest such society west of the Mississippi River. The upheaval of the Civil War and the years after caused it to flounder. It was revived in 1880 and has continued to the present.

Chapter 6: For the full story of the donation, movement and ultimate restoration of #463, see Antoinette Gibbons's *The Story of the Cumbres & Toltec Scenic RR and Engine No. 463* (Longmont, CO: RAB Enterprises Inc., 1995). Other material for this chapter came from the *Hometown Herald*, commission files, the *C&TSRR Dispatch* and Friends of the C&TSRR files.

Chapter 7: Testimony to the Friends of the C&TSRR doing careful restoration work is taken from Gibbons (1995), cited earlier. Other material for this chapter came from the *C&TSRR Dispatch* 2, no. 4 (December 1989) and vol. 4, no. 1 (March 1991) and *Locomotive & Railway Preservation* (July–August 1988).

Chapter 8: Bill Lock's quotes at the chapter's end came from the *C&TSRR Dispatch* 8, no. 3 (Fall 1995). Other material for this chapter came from commission files, the *C&TSRR Dispatch* and Victor J. Stone's *Taking Stock: Narrow Gauge Stock Cars of the Denver & Rio Grande, 1873–1968* (N.p.: Creedstone Publications, 1992), as well as Friends of the C&TSRR files and *Trans-Action*, published by the UTLX Company.

Chapter 9: Regarding the Colorado Historical Society's award to the Friends, it also might be remembered that in 1994, the State of New Mexico awarded the Friends a Heritage Preservation Award for its restoration work on the railroad. See the *C&TS Dispatch* (May 1994) and vol. 10, no. 2 (Summer 1997). For testimony on the Friends work on a grand scale and with a strong emphasis on cooperation, see the spring 1999 issue of *Railway Magazine Quarterly*, the journal of the Association of Railway Museums (Aaron Issacs, editor). Other material for this chapter came from the *C&TS Dispatch* and commission files.

Chapter 10: Material for this chapter came from the *C&TSRR Dispatch* and commission files.

Chapter 11: Material for this chapter came from the *New Mexico Railroader*, Friends files, commission files and the *Albuquerque Journal North*.

Epilogue: Material for this chapter came from commission files, Friends files and the *Albuquerque Journal North*.

ABOUT THE AUTHOR AND PHOTOGRAPHER

Spencer Wilson has been a board member of both the Cumbres & Toltec Scenic Railroad and the former Cumbres & Toltec Scenic Railroad Commission. He has also been a board member of the Historical Society of New Mexico, New Mexico Architectural Foundation, New Mexico Endowment for the Humanities and New Mexico Book League, among many other involvements. He taught at the New Mexico Institute of Mining and Technology for more than two decades. He twice served as president of the Historical Society of New Mexico and also served as president of the Socorro County Historical Society.

Wes Pfarner is the photography archivist of the Friends of the Cumbres & Toltec Scenic Railroad.

Visit us at
www.historypress.net